For my grandchildren:
Michael, Paul, Sofia, Marissa, and Gianna

THE
ACHILLES
HEEL

THE
ACHILLES
HEEL

A Citizen's Guide to
Understanding and
Closing the Black-White
Academic Achievement
Gap in Our Schools

MICHAEL J. BAKALIS

Harbridge Press
Woodridge, Illinois

The Achilles Heel: A Citizen's Guide to Understanding and Closing the Black-White Academic Achievement Gap in Our Schools
Copyright © 2013 by Michael J. Bakalis

International Standard Book Number: 978-0-9830030-6-9
Library of Congress Control Number: 2013934064

Printed in the United States of America

Harbridge Press
Woodridge, Illinois
www.harbridgepress.com

TABLE OF CONTENTS

THE ACHILLES HEEL

In Greek mythology the story is told that when the warrior Achilles was an infant, his mother was informed by one who could foresee the future that her child would be killed in battle. Seeking a way to prevent the prediction from coming to pass, Achilles' mother took the child to the River Styx, which was said to have magical powers of invincibility, and, holding her son by the heels, she dipped his body into the water. All of his body, except for his heels, was covered by this mysterious water.

As a grown man, Achilles became a courageous warrior and survived numerous battles. During the Trojan War, however, a poisonous arrow struck him in his heel, and he was killed. From that mythical story has come down to us the concept of "The Achilles Heel," which is meant as a metaphor for a fatal weakness in something that otherwise possesses overall strength. I believe that in our great American educational system, the seemingly unfixable academic achievement gap between white and black students is our nation's Achilles Heel.

There are, of course, many different achievement gaps. Hispanic students are behind whites on test scores, and Native Americans fare even worse. There is another achievement gap that few people seem to worry about—the gap between high-achieving Asian-American students and lower-achieving white, black, Hispanic, and Native American students. So why is the black-white achievement gap the potential Achilles Heel and not the others?

As I explored that phenomenon, I found the basic reason is that history, slavery, discrimination, poverty, and now technological advances have, at different stages of our history, kept African-Americans out of the mainstream of American progress and development. Certainly many have moved into the world of middle-class America; however, a small but significant segment today lives in urban and suburban ghettos and in an isolated world with lifestyles and values far different from those of most Americans. Their environment is one of idle men on street corners; gang-bangers selling drugs on other corners; high numbers of out-of-wedlock births; few employment options; poverty; and streets littered with papers, cups, and junk. Add to that neighborhoods that are scenes of violent crime. It is on these streets that the young must travel from their homes to their schools. The chances of most of these young people accessing the American Dream range from slim, even with an average education, to virtually none with the academic achievement levels they are scoring on state academic assessments.

There are other reasons as well to focus on the black-white achievement gap. As I explore in subsequent chapters, it is not only poor urban underclass black children who are not achieving academically, but it is also black middle-class students. And it is not only African-American students who are falling behind but also black students in England, the Netherlands, France, Germany, Australia, and Canada. How can we explain this? I explore various answers that have been put forth and attempt to assess the validity of those explanations in the chapters that follow.

Unfortunately, there are too few honest discussions about race in our country. Rational dialogue seems to quickly deteriorate into charges of racism from one side or the other. We desperately need these discussions between black and white Americans so that we can jointly develop strategies that can equalize opportunities in a just way for all Americans. We need some straight talk about race, and I have tried to provide that in this book. I believe this is the only way we can finally find some real workable answers for doing what we can to narrow the differences in the achievement of black and white young people.

Many scholarly books and articles have been written about the achievement gap, but few offer workable solutions to the problem. I have put forth some ideas to close that gap. These ideas are based on a career in education and government that has spanned more than four decades of working in schools, especially in inner-city African-American communities. Some of the ideas I have suggested are bold, perhaps even radical. But the state of academic achievement in the African-American community is, in my mind, so serious that Band-Aids will no longer work. Too many generations have been lost, and the time to act is long past. A failure to act boldly will result in dire consequences because the situation is a social time-bomb capable of igniting at any time. Our strong educational system, which has made us an economic and military power in the world, has a small vulnerable part that could shake the foundation of the entire educational enterprise. The black-white achievement gap could very well be our Achilles Heel.

CHAPTER 1

WHERE WE ARE

In the second decade of the twenty-first century, America remains the greatest economic and military power on the planet. An economic downturn in the nation, a growing economic crisis in Europe, and the growth of the economy in China threaten to undermine that leadership status, but America, with all its challenges, continues to remain the world leader. Another threat, though, perhaps not as dramatic as the economic, ideological, and military clash of nations, presents a challenge to American pre-eminence. That threat is the problem with American education.

Today our educational system stands as a key to the nation's economic and military success. Contrary to commonly held assumptions, education has not held that crucial position in America's past. In the previous eras of the agricultural and industrial economies, education played but a limited role. The American West was won by little-educated but courageous and hard-driving pioneers. America's rise to industrial prominence was achieved not by college educated-leaders but rather by business giants such as John D. Rockefeller, Cornelius Vanderbilt, and Andrew Carnegie, men of limited formal education but of limitless vision and drive. The men and women who worked the factory lines and sweatshops were often uneducated blacks and European immigrants. That world is long gone today. The knowledge, information, service economy world of today cannot function without an educated, problem-solving, analytical, collaborative workforce. High school dropouts of a generation or two ago did not face a certain life of failure. Jobs were available in factories and steel mills across the nation. Now large numbers of those factories and steel mills are gone. Today's high school dropouts, or even graduates, who lack basic language, writing, and mathematical skills have few, if any, options. Without subsequent generations of educated Americans, the prospect of American decline will not only be a possibility but, in fact, an inevitability.

The problem of American education is a curious one. Surveys of Americans reveal that, on the whole, Americans are very satisfied with their local schools. Across the globe students from Europe, Asia, and Africa and beyond compete to be admitted to American universities to pursue their professional studies. It is also clear that America's position of being the leading economic and military power in the world could hardly have occurred with a dysfunctional or failed educational system. Yet in spite of these successes and public approval, our federal government, state governments, private foundations, and politicians of both parties all advocate various programs, strategies, and initiatives to "reform" American education. The schools, we are told, are clearly not doing their job, and the numbers vividly underscore the complaint. American students, statistics reveal, do not score well on international assessments in comparison with other students in foreign lands. The American high school dropout rate is a national disgrace as most of our major large-city school systems graduate only 40 percent to 60 percent of the students who enrolled as freshmen; the percentages for some minority students who fail to graduate has now reached 70 percent to 80 percent in some cities.

In order to understand this strange American duality about schools more fully—both approving school performance and celebrating the success that system has brought us as a nation while simultaneously sounding the trumpet for school reform—one must look somewhat to the past to understand today. From the mid-nineteenth century with the establishment of the American Common School, which was a compulsory, tax-supported, nonsectarian institution open to all, school reform has been an ever constant feature of how Americans view their schools. The establishment of a truly public education system, led by leaders such as Horace Mann, Henry Barnard, and many others, was itself a major reform of huge importance. What had been for two hundred years a hodgepodge of semipublic, private, home, and sectarian schools with voluntary attendance was transformed into a system that possessed all the elements that we today understand to be the essence of American public education. The Common School Crusade reform, as major and profound as it was, was only the beginning of a never-ending stream of ideas, projects, and movements to reform that newly established common school system—and then to reform the reforms. As America changed from an agricultural to an industrial society and then, in our own time, to a service-, information-, knowledge-based economy, calls, at each step along the way, were made to reform the schools. Those who have been in education as students, teachers, or policy makers have witnessed a never-ending implementation of school reforms. In the 1950s Arthur Bestor complained of *Educational Wastelands*, Charles Silberman wrote about the *Crisis in the Classroom* in the 1970s, and James Koerner described the *Miseducation of American Teachers* in the 1960s. The U.S. Department of Education prodded the states to reform with its dramatic and influential report "A Nation at Risk" in the 1980s. President George W. Bush expanded the reform role of the federal government with his "No Child Left Behind" policy in the beginning of this century, moving even beyond Lyndon Johnson's Elementary and Secondary Schools Act of the 1960s. President Obama continued this quest for reform with his "Race to the Top" policy initiative. Advocates of introducing market forces into what in effect has been a quasi-monopoly of public education have changed the educational landscape with the introduction of charter schools and school vouchers. And yet, even with one reform initiative following another, the calls for school reform remain multiple, loud, and forceful today. But how justified are these continuous calls for school reform? Are American schools really that bad? Or is there something else operating here that clouds our picture of American public schools?

Perhaps the most accurate answer to those questions is that America's schools are good for most, great for a few, and miserable for others. The statistical comparison of American students with foreign students of a similar age at first glance tells a troubling story. The Organization For Economic Cooperation and Development (OECD) monitors social and economic facts for the thirty-two richest nations in the world. They administer the Programme for International Student Assessment (PISA). In that assessment the United States was ranked fifteenth. Additional results from the OECD assessment found the U.S. high school graduation rates near the bottom of the list. The results in scientific literacy were equally disheartening as U.S. students ranked twenty-first of thirty nations. A similar troubling result was reported in the areas of math literacy and problem-solving ability, in which U.S. students scored twenty-fifth of thirty nations and twenty-fourth of twenty-nine countries, respectively. Of equal concern was the mistaken conception American students have of their own abilities. When American thirteen-year-olds were asked whether they believed they were good at doing math, 68 percent said they were. In reality American students placed dead last in the mathematics test. Korean students were in first place, even though, when asked that same question, only 23 percent of those students said they were "good at math."

On the United States test, the National Assessment of Educational Progress (NAEP), the negative results continued. The NAEP ranks students in relation to four levels: Below Basic, Basic, Proficient, and Advanced. On this test one quarter of American students did poorly in reading: one-fourth were Below Basic. In geography, math, and civics one-third were Below Basic, while 57 percent were at the Basic level only in history. And even when these students do graduate from high school, too many are clearly unprepared to be successful at college work. Today 40 percent of all students entering college as freshman need remedial courses to acquire the skills and knowledge that will enable them to complete and succeed in subsequent college credit work. The additional cost of these catch-up courses is estimated to be in excess of two billion dollars every year. When college instructors are interviewed, more than 70 percent report that the students they teach do not understand complex reading assignments, almost 60 percent say students have no concept of how to do research, and 55 percent cannot apply knowledge to solve problems. Sixty-five percent of college instructors say students do not possess basic work and study habits and cannot write an acceptable paragraph.

Certainly the cumulative effect of these results and reports about American student academic achievement is cause for great concern. But are they cause for national panic? Do they signal that American education is in need of some fundamental change? The true answer can be found if we dig a bit deeper into those numbers. What seems to be the situation is that schools are actually functioning quite well for some students. Certainly some changes are needed, but American public education is not an idea or institution that is the failure some alarmists would have us believe. Some changes are needed for all of our students, and all of our students need to achieve at higher levels if our nation is to compete successfully in the ever-changing global economy. Students who are not succeeding in our educational system and students whom the educational system is failing are our African-American minority students. Students who continue, decade after decade and generation after generation, to be unable to benefit from many American schools are too many of the nation's African-American young men and women.

Why focus on black kids, some might ask. What about Hispanics, Native Americans, and other minorities? The miseducation of Native Americans would require another entire book, and Hispanics seem to be on an educational path that was followed earlier by numerous white ethnic groups who preceded them as immigrant school children. It has been a journey that, as yet, has not led to widespread educational success for Hispanics, but it still follows closely the educational journey followed by Polish, Italian, Greek, Russian, Jewish, and Scandinavian immigrants who succeeded in previous decades. (I will explore this theme further in Chapter II.)

The situation for our black students is different. Millions, if not billions, of dollars have been spent by individual schools, local school districts, states, private foundations, and the federal government on strategies, programs, and special initiatives to assist black students so that they might be academically successful. Some of those dollars have had the desired effect, but in most cases we have seen little return for the money spent. Today a major educational goal of the nation is to close the academic "achievement gap." This achievement gap is not a new or recent development. It has, with some minor exceptions, existed in all of American history, but we, as a nation, have not yet found the answer to closing that gap. Another look at the numbers reveals a special concern about the low achievement scores.

The fact that American students do not rank at the top or near the top in international subject matter assessments is a fact that cannot be disputed. Those results certainly tell us that all is not well with American education, and we must act to do better. Digging deeper into those numbers sounds an even more serious alarm, one with no immediate solution in sight. The numbers that are most troubling are those that chart the progress of African-American students. The academic performance of black students on all standardized tests is worse than any other racial or ethnic group. The average African-American student who is seventeen years old has NAEP scores in basic subjects such as reading, math, and science that are the equivalent of thirteen–year-old white students. In math, 70 percent of black students scored at Below Basic levels, and in science 75 percent of black students also scored at the Below Basic level. By the end of high school, black students perform at the level of white seventh graders in knowledge of U.S. history. While critics decry the performance of American students on the Third International Mathematics and Science Study (TIMSS) test, when one looks at the levels of achievement by racial groups, a similar story of black underachievement is revealed.

In that TIMSS assessment American white students scored in the upper third in math of the thirty-nine nations taking the test and sixth from the top in the science category. American black students were near the bottom in math, thirty-first of thirty-nine, and they had the same score and ranking in science. Since white students were 65 percent of all students taking the test, they actually scored well against the other thirty-eight nations. A similar disheartening note is found when we look at the racial achievement results on the Programme for International Student Assessment (PISA). In that assessment, which was taken by some twenty-eight to thirty-two nations, American white students scored second of twenty-nine nations, while American black students ranked twenty-sixth of twenty-nine nations taking the test. Similar achievement gaps were evident in the math and science portions of the exam. In the math section, whites scored seventh out of thirty nations, while our black students scored twenty-seventh out of thirty nations. In science a similar story was revealed as American white students scored fourth of the thirty nations taking the test, while American black students ranked twenty-seventh out of those same nations.

The record of African-American students is no better on state level assessments or on the Scholastic Aptitude Test (SAT) and American College Test (ACT) assessments used for college admissions. The percent of blacks who met the readiness standard in reading on the ACT was an exceptionally low 4 percent in 2011. On the Massachusetts state test taken by all of that state's students, 80 percent of African-American students failed the exam. The Massachusetts figure is hardly the exception. In every single state an achievement gap in reading is evident between white and black students; there is no state in which black students outperformed white students. The gap ranged from the lowest in Hawaii to the highest in Wisconsin, with reading and math differences between the races ranging from twenty-six to thirty-one points.

The high school dropout rate is one affecting American students of every race and ethnic origin but none more so than minority students. Too many urban school districts over the years have reported dropout numbers in various forms and often created ways to mask the growing failure of their schools. More precise statistics today report the dropout rate in Houston as somewhere between 45 percent and 75 percent; a similar range is true for Chicago, Philadelphia, New York, Los Angeles, Washington D.C., and other major cities. Today certain schools that boast of sending 100 percent of their graduating class to college fail to mention that 25 percent to 50 percent of the students that started as freshmen with that same graduating class had long ago dropped out of school. Such schools manage to receive favorable television and newspaper coverage about their successes—a strange boast when the schools have lost a large percentage of the students they originally enrolled.

The cost to society of dropouts of any race or color is high; those costs come in the form of unemployment, welfare payments, food stamps, crime costs, and prison incarceration. Chicago figures underscore the high cost of dropout rates: in 2010 48 percent of dropouts between the ages of eighteen and sixty-four did not work a single week in a year. Fifteen percent of young dropouts aged eighteen to thirty-four were in prison in 2010; for black male dropouts the figure was a staggering 29 percent. The impact of a high school diploma is evident when one discovers that the incarceration rate for black males who have graduated from high school drops to 8 percent, and to only 1 percent when African-American men have a college degree.

In the past three decades Americans have spent millions of dollars for public education and have put forth one initiative after another and a new reform that followed closely on the heels of the previous reform. Yet the test scores show that American student performance has changed little during that thirty-year period. Today's schools may be classified as bad, poor, or mediocre by some, but they are not worse or more mediocre than before. The national average scores on the SAT and high school graduation rates have remained essentially the same during that time period. All the previously cited bad news about American schools and the black-white achievement gap does not mean that our educational system is on the verge of collapse. As poor as some of the NAEP test scores might seem, they have actually risen slightly in the past two decades. Today 84 percent of Americans aged twenty-five and older have a high school diploma compared to only about 25 percent of that same age group in 1940. More Americans have access to two- and four-year colleges than ever before in our history, and more Americans than ever before are enrolling in those institutions. The American educational journey of providing educational opportunity and access to schooling at every level has been a resounding success story.

The quantity of our education has been our token of great achievement, but it is the quality of that education for all persons that remains our elusive goal. Many years ago then Secretary of Health, Education and Welfare John Gardner eloquently summed up our unique American situation in his book, *Excellence*, when he posed the question we have yet to answer: Can we be equal and excellent, too? That remains the central question as we attempt to understand and close the academic achievement gap in America's schools. Harvard educator Tony Wagner has written, "The problem is not the 'failure' of our public schools. They are not incrementally better or worse than they were fifty years ago. They haven't really changed for the better or worse. The world has changed. That's the real problem." No doubt Wagner is correct as he views all of American public education, but is he correct when we consider the story of American blacks in our educational system? The world has certainly changed for black Americans in the past fifty years. No signs tell blacks which restaurants they are forbidden to enter or which drinking fountains they can use. No American state governor dares block a black student's admission to a state university. American blacks fill professional positions as physicians, lawyers, college professors, school teachers, and corporate CEOs. An African-American has been elected president of the United States. Yet as barrier after barrier of racial discrimination has fallen and as unprecedented opportunities now are available to young black men and women, the academic achievement barrier for far too many young blacks seems to remain unbreakable. Why does this situation continue to exist? Why are there so many questionable theories and explanations for the black-white achievement gap? Why can't we seem to close that gap?

To some these questions may seem to be overdramatizing the situation. After all, more than two-thirds of African-Americans are part of the American middle class. They are not in poverty. They don't reside in ghettos. They are not part of the black-on-black shootings that plague our inner-city neighborhoods. They don't receive welfare or food stamps, and they didn't all achieve their respectable and successful middle- and upper-class economic status because of affirmative action policies. Still, even their children, as we shall see in later chapters of this book, are not doing as well as they should in our schools.

Those students must concern us but others even more so. Only about 16 percent of public school students in grades K-12 go to urban schools in cities of 250,000 or more. About 12 percent of the nation's students almost all of whom are black and Hispanic go to those urban schools, and estimates are that about 10 percent of our students go to what are considered our worst schools. That may not seem like a large number, but in terms of the potential consequences of how students of these schools will live their lives, those small numbers have enormous consequences for our nation.

Recalling the ancient Greek myth, when the great warrior Achilles was born, it was foretold that he would die in battle. To prevent this prediction from happening the new infant's mother took the child to the River Styx, which was reputed to have special powers that could make an individual invincible. She placed her infant son in the water so that it covered his entire body but did not wash over the heel of his foot.

During the Trojan War, Achilles, who had survived numerous battles before, was struck in his heel by a poison arrow and killed. While the majority of his body was strong and invincible, this one vulnerable spot caused his downfall. The black-white achievement gap is the Achilles Heel of American education. Our schools, while needing some change, are fundamentally strong. That change must and will come, although the process is painfully slow. American schools have never been the change agents of our society. Rather, they have responded to and have been mirrors of large-scale American social, economic, and political changes. As the nation became more democratic, so, too, did the schools. As the economy shifted from an agricultural to an industrial base, so, too, did the schools respond to that change. Today as we are transforming into a knowledge, service, information, digital global economy, the schools will eventually follow. Unless we can confront, address, and solve the black-white academic achievement gap, though, African-American young people will be left behind, unable to compete and survive in this new global, high-tech world.

Over the decades American schools have changed, yet African-American underachievement has remained a constant feature of our schools. It will be, unless resolved, the Achilles Heel of our educational system and could threaten to undermine the institution of American public education as we have known it.

In the chapters that follow we will seek first an understanding of this achievement gap. Unless we can with some assurance define the problem, we are unlikely to find the correct solutions. Secondly, we will explore possible solutions—a few perhaps more radical than some would want. But we have already attempted more traditional, safer routes, and they have led us nowhere. It is important, however, to look back briefly at some educational history. Too often we Americans seem to suffer from historical amnesia, sometimes thinking that every situation is new. We grapple for answers when previous generations have already confronted and attempted to solve the same or similar issues. A common argument one hears today goes somewhat as follows: Millions of immigrants came to this country from various parts of Europe and Asia with no knowledge of the English language, no understanding of our culture, and no wealth of any kind. They lived in isolated, impoverished ghetto neighborhoods, yet with all the obstacles they faced, these people—some with a different skin color, strange names, different religions, unfamiliar languages, and different customs—made it in America. Their children succeeded in American schools and went on to find success in virtually every field imaginable. If they did it, the argument goes, and more recently if Asian and East Indian children are succeeding today, why can't African-Americans, who have been in our country for more than four hundred years and have no language barriers, do it today? Yes, the argument continues, there were slavery and discrimination, but what is the rationale or excuse for underachievement now? We begin this journey of discovery by looking first at the essence of the above argument to see how these poor, non-English speaking immigrants fared in our schools. Then we explore whether there are lessons to be learned from that experience that may have relevance for our quest for answers to the current black-white achievement gap.

CHAPTER II

SOME LESSONS FROM THE PAST

Until the middle years of the nineteenth century it is incorrect to speak of the American Educational System. In fact, from the first European settlement in 1607 until the mid-nineteenth century, there was no single public educational system in the nation. A mixture of no schooling at all, home schooling, quasi-public schooling, and mostly private and sectarian schooling characterized the educational landscape available to American children for well over the first two hundred years of European settlement in America. For American Negroes, their bondage into slavery meant no formal education whatsoever, a condition codified into laws. For more than two centuries, the two key assumptions that are the foundation of American education today—compulsory student attendance and tax-supported schools to which everyone must contribute—were rarely, if ever, discussed and found no real advocates or support. It was only through the social and political movement known as the Common School Crusade, advanced by the courageous efforts of public school advocates in various states during the early nineteenth century, that these two key ideas found fertile ground for acceptance

These two key elements of today's public school system faced enormous obstacles. It was generally believed by most Americans that the education of children was primarily a family and parental function, with religious institutions serving in a complementary role. The notion that a government entity, such as a state, could legislatively take away parental authority and, by law, force a child to attend school was rejected by almost everyone. To further require all adults, whether or not they had children, to pay taxes to support the education of not only their own children but other people's children as well was viewed as a most radical and unacceptable idea. As was discussed in the previous chapter, the necessity for a person to have an education was also not widely supported. America seemed to be growing and prospering quite well without a highly-educated population. It is helpful to remember that in 1910 only 10 percent of Americans had attended secondary schools; by 1940 only 40 percent of Americans had graduated from high school. Half of all adults in 1900 had never reached eighth grade. Of those who did start high school in New York and Boston in the 1940s, more than half failed to graduate; few people cared, however, because the concept of school dropout as a societal problem had not entered the American discussion.

As was mentioned earlier, those majorities who never finished eighth grade or high school could generally find employment, raise a family, buy a home, take family vacations, and lead a good middle-class life. So if education was only minimally important to a person's realizing the American Dream, what role did the schools play in the lives of black and immigrant children in the nineteenth and early twentieth centuries? Can we find some clues to the contemporary refrain, "If poor, non-English-speaking immigrant kids could make it in our schools, why can't blacks do the same thing?"

It is important to underscore the fact that the end of slavery for American Negroes did not mean the end of widespread discrimination and racial oppression. Until the late nineteenth and early twentieth centuries, the majority of blacks remained concentrated in the southern states of the old Confederacy. The enthusiasm of the newly freed slaves for education was great, but it quickly disappeared among the realities of southern racism and segregation. Racially segregated schools, made legal by the U.S. Supreme Court's *Plessey v. Ferguson* decision, resulted in totally inadequate school facilities for black students, lax enforcement of school attendance laws, and great disparities in funding. For example, in one southern county in 1912, one dollar per pupil was spent for black education, and $33.40 was spent for every white child. The western and northern states were almost as opposed to the schooling of blacks as was the South. Even the so-called industrial schools in the South were poorly supported because whites feared that trained blacks would compete with whites for their jobs. The economic growth of the industrial North served as a magnet for poor, un-educated blacks who saw job opportunities and few legal racial restrictions on them in the North. Thus began a massive population movement of southern blacks to the urban centers of the North. In those cities, at least in the early years, Negroes did not en-counter racially segregated schools, but, rather, black children sat side by side with white children, who were increasingly the children of immigrants from a variety of southern and eastern European nations. Whether in Providence, Rhode Island, or Chicago, Illinois, these children from different races and na-tionalities received the same education. So how did each group do? The answer, contrary to widely held assumptions, was that both black children and their white immigrant classmates did not do too well.

The facts are that the first generation of immigrant children did not find widespread success in American schools. The New York state legislature desegregated its schools in 1900, so children of all backgrounds sat in the same classrooms. Immigrant children seemed to succeed or fail at different rates according to their ethnic origin, but none did particularly well in the sense that they graduated or achieved at their recommended grade/age level. Black students, Mexicans, and Italians did not fare well in schools. Jews, Greeks, and Chinese origin students did better although not at exceptionally impressive rates. In studies begun in 1898 in urban centers, results indicated more children failed in school than succeeded. Even in the earliest years of the twentieth century, school officials complained about Negro children in their schools. A New York study reported that the behavior of Negro children was not "immoral" but "unmoral," such as that of an ignorant and naïve child. This 1911 survey spoke to the poor performance of black students and placed the blame on the lack of authority, broken homes, and the working mothers in black families. Immigrants were doing no better than blacks in the schools. By the 1940s, New York schools had instituted remedial programs for poor immigrant Italian children, but the general issue of poor academic achievement among blacks was defined as a "Negro problem." The depth of racism found even in the North was illustrated in the early years of the twentieth century in New York City when black poverty was characterized as "blackness" and not simply as poverty. In effect, the urban schools were failing everyone—black and white. Dropouts were the rule, not the exception. The difference for white children was that they were more quickly absorbed into the economy, while black dropouts went to the back of the economic job lines. The failure of children in schools was reported by the Dillingham Commission, which concluded that 29 percent of native white students, 34 percent of immigrant students, and 53 percent of black students were "retarded," the word used to classify children who were older than normal for the grades they were in.

The work of Michael Homel in his book *Down From Equality* and Kathryn Neckerman in her book *Schools Betrayed* provide important case study insights regarding black and white education in the first part of the twentieth century in the urban setting of Chicago. In 1900 the schools of Chicago were not racially segregated, and school attendance was on the rise. By 1915 only one school had a black enrollment of more than 90 percent. Overall attendance grew by more than 20 percent for the entire system, primarily because of Chicago's general population growth as well as the large influx of southern and eastern European immigrants. The growth figure for black school enrollment was, in fact, staggering, as attendance for that group increased more 185 percent. Clearly, black southern migrant enthusiasm for education was great. The Chicago Board of Education had hired black teachers as early as the 1880s, so conditions seemed good for children of all backgrounds to be educated well, even though in these early years some schools had as many as forty to sixty students in an elementary class.

Yet as the decades progressed, the situation in the schools did not get better; rather, it became worse. In 1910 the schools of Chicago counted 1 percent of their students as black. By 1930 that figure reached 5 percent, and by 1960 it rose to 40 percent. By the 1930s the condition of blacks in the schools was rapidly changing. Black education in Chicago was characterized by increased segregation, overcrowding, and lack of needed financial resources. The Great Depression hurt all Americans, but it was particularly devastating to Chicago Negroes. In 1934 three-fifths of black women and four-fifths of black men were unemployed. By 1934 46 percent of black families were receiving public assistance. As late as 1940, more than 30 percent of blacks were on relief or unemployed. Because of the lack of work or labor force discrimination against blacks, Negro students often stayed in school longer than their white counterparts. This absence of work options and their parents' lack of education probably served as incentives for not readily dropping out of school. Among adult blacks eighteen and older in 1934, only one-fourth of men and one-third of women had gone to school beyond the eighth grade.

While black students may have been forced by circumstances to remain in school longer, remaining there did not positively impact their academic achievement. Although evidence of achievement on standardized tests is limited, what facts we do have reveal that in the 1930s black students did poorly on tests and were often two to three years behind in their grade levels. Immigrant children also did poorly, and, in fact, blacks did slightly better than their white immigrant classmates. The majority of black students were from the South and were demoted from two to four grades because of their poor academic performance. As the proportion of black students in Chicago increased, so, too, did the achievement disparity between black and white students. In 1915 only 8 percent of Chicago students attended a 90 percent or all-black school. By 1930 that percentage had risen from 8 percent to 84 percent. By 1940 brand new young teachers, fresh out of college, were teaching at 40 percent of black schools while only 22 percent of those newly graduated teachers were at white ethnic schools.

Other aspects of our current urban school environment also developed in the period from 1930 to 1960. The prominent black newspaper *The Defender* reported that school violence was on the rise. A woman teacher was pushed up against the wall and threatened, and another report spoke of students throwing acid on a teacher. Another story reported that a teacher had forcibly taken a gun from a student but was then forced to return the weapon when the student threatened the teacher with a knife. In

1929 two Negro teachers reported that their black students "have a general antagonistic attitude toward everything pertaining to school." Another teacher complained that "more time is spent enforcing the simple habits of control than anything else." Such comments would seem very contemporary to teachers working in Chicago public schools more than eighty years later.

What would be different, however, is the family structure of the students. In 1920 more than 85 percent of all Chicago students, black and white, lived in two-parent homes. That figure remained relatively constant over the next four decades: 83.6 percent in 1940 and 83.1 percent in 1960. Nevertheless, with the element so often cited today of one-parent families being a contributing factor in school academic and disciple problems mostly absent in those earlier decades, black children at that time still did not do well in school. In 1964 a Chicago school study showed one-third of ninth graders in black high schools were in basic English classes created for students who were three or more years below grade level. Compare this with fewer than 5 percent of students in that same grade who were in predominantly white schools. That same study reported that 40 percent of all classes in low-income black schools were taught at the basic level while only 10 percent of all classes were taught at that low level in predominantly white schools.

Chicago school history is one of increasing disparity in academic achievement of black and white students as the percentage of black students increased in the school system. The city responded to this issue in essentially three ways: First, the schools became increasingly segregated by race. No law created this situation, but residential patterns and public policy did. Official and unofficial real estate practices kept blacks in certain communities on the south and west sides of the city. Public policy created high-rise housing projects, which also kept blacks in particular parts of Chicago. The result was increasingly segregated schools and increasing social isolation of the African-American community. A second response was to move to vocational education as a solution for those students who were not succeeding in the more academic curriculum tracks. In fact, three unforeseen things diluted the results of this policy response to the growing problem of black underachievement. First, white ethnics, who faced little opposition or discrimination in the industrial factory workplace, benefited more from the programs because they were the first to fill the available jobs. . Blacks saw little incentive to participate in the programs because they realized they probably would be the last to be hired once they entered the labor force. The second problem with this vocational school initiative arose over time because of the public perception that these programs were created for blacks, who could not succeed in the regular academic courses. Increasingly, by the end of the last century, African-Americans were rejecting vocational education as a degrading, second-class, racist option that they did not want. The third general response to the growing achievement gap was one that continues to this day: the institution of remedial education for low-achieving students. In earlier decades it took the form of specialized tracked classes and the withholding of grade promotion from students.

In *Schools Betrayed*, author Kathryn Neckerman makes the following statement: "Urban schools," she writes," were never designed to produce equality of achievement." Yet isn't this exactly what the movement to close the black-white achievement gap is all about? If Neckerman has her school history correct, and I believe she does, what were and are the public schools meant to do? American schools, from the very beginning of becoming the public school system we have today, were meant to provide one fundamental goal: equality of opportunity. Equality of opportunity is quite different from equality of results. Give everyone an equal chance, the American creed proclaims, and those with ability, drive, determination, ambition, and plain hard work can succeed. If today some set the goal as equality of results, that is a new goal and one that clearly runs counter to the value of individual initiative that has previously characterized the American experience.

So what conclusions or lessons can we identify from this brief overview of American educational history, and what relevance does any of this have for this important issue of the black-white achievement gap? One obvious lesson is that for most of our history, Americans have been most concerned with the issue of access to education and not equal results for all children. No one was seriously discussing or very concerned about the achievement gap between native white students and the Italian, Jewish, Greek, Polish, or Russian immigrant children who arrived between 1880 to 1960. If any explanations were offered at all, they were often genetic in nature—these immigrant children just weren't very smart. It was really only in the 1970s and 1980s that a strong national dialogue began to discuss not only the *quantity* of education available to Americans but, for the first time, a serious discussion of the *quality* of schooling as well.

Another lesson from our historical experience relates directly to the question we suggested is being posed by some today: "If the European immigrants who came here in poverty without knowing the English language could succeed in our schools, why can't today's black students do the same?" The historically correct response to that question is simple: "What you are assuming happened, in fact, never happened." What really happened is that overwhelming numbers of first-generation immigrant children failed in school, or, more accurately, the schools failed them. The statistics recording the rates at which immigrant young people left school and failed to graduate underscore the fact that while some of that generation did benefit, graduate, and go on to higher socio-economic levels, most did not. So if we imagine some golden age in which the schools worked for students of all ethnic and racial backgrounds, we are dealing with fantasy and not American history. What really happened is that only after various immigrant groups had attained some level of economic stability, security, and language proficiency did their children (often the second, not the first generation) find that the schools could be vehicles for success and upward mobility. Increasingly as the decades after 1900 wore on, it became clear that students' academic success was consistently dependent on the socio-economic position and stability of the family. As compulsory attendance levels were increased to higher grade levels, the failure rate for all students was pushed into the upper grades in Chicago, New York, Detroit, Philadelphia, and Washington D.C. Certainly this seems to be a forgotten episode for those who today seek to stem the dropout rate and close the achievement gap by advocating raising the compulsory school attendance age to eighteen.

Specifically in regard to African-American students, a number of things stand out from our past history. The first is that they began their entrance into American public schools at an enormous disadvantage. Two hundred fifty years of being held in slavery meant that there was no strong tradition or model of academic achievement. Jim Crow laws and deeply institutionalized racism and discrimination signaled to black students that school achievement had no real payoff. Where could they go and what could they really do with a good education? Facing racism and discrimination every day of their lives, their conclusion was clear—there really was no incentive or payoff in American society as it existed. The mass migration of southern blacks to the North seemed for a brief moment to offer some hope, because schools there were not legally segregated and even employed some black teachers. But as the movement of blacks from the South to northern cities accelerated and their percentages in the schools became larger, conditions deteriorated, schools became more segregated by neighborhoods, and black communities became more isolated. Chicago noted a 65 percent increase in so-called underprivileged children between 1924 and 1931. Although black children often stayed in school longer than white children, that extra time did not translate into grade attainment equal to whites who did remain in their classes. Blacks consistently had higher levels of grade retardation, meaning they were one, two, or more years behind where they should have been. The grade point averages of black students were consistently lower than those of white students, and even though they remained in school longer than many whites, the average white immigrant students still eventually completed more grades than the average black students. Patterns of black student attitudes and behavior that are evident in many black students today were evident and documented in the 1920s, 1930s, and 1940s.

Thus, in looking for answers to today's academic achievement gap and student dropout rate, we are forced to conclude that we cannot depend on our past history to answer the challenges we face today. There is little comfort in the realization that many problems we face today were present forty, fifty, eighty, and even one hundred years ago. Today the bar has been set higher for our educational system. We remain committed to the goal of equal opportunity for all students, and though we do not formally articulate it, the nation is calling for equality of results as well. Concrete evidence of this was President George W. Bush's No Child Left Behind educational initiative, which called for the ambitious, and some would say unrealistic, goal of having all students, rich and poor, black, brown, yellow, red, or white, achieve equal educational attainment by the year 2014. This is what the concern and debate surrounding the black-white achievement gap are all about. Thus far, no person or program has found the answer to how to close that gap, partly because the problem itself has been defined in so many different ways. It is important, then, that we clearly define the problem itself before we seek to offer any realistic solutions.

For some, the core of the problem is money: Just give more financial resources to these underachieving schools, they argue, and those students will really have equal opportunity and will do well. To others, the problem is simple: Poverty is the culprit. If we take kids out of poverty, they will achieve academically. Still others see the problem as an issue of family structure and stability. The issue, as they define it, is that for large numbers of inner-city black children, dysfunctional or non-existent families are the rule and not the exception. Fix the family foundation, they argue, and kids will succeed. Some say that racism remains the key element. Discrimination, they claim, is present every day in the life of every black student. They see and feel it in their schools. The numbers, they believe, confirm it in black student suspension and expulsion rates, and they see it among the high numbers of unemployed youth and the inordinately high numbers of young blacks who populate our prisons. Yet another group of writers place the blame on culture. Poor blacks, they say, are living in what has come to be known as a culture of poverty, a separate and distinct way of looking at the world, the future, and the values one holds as part of one's personal make-up and conduct. That culture must be changed, they say, or nothing else will likely ever change. And finally there are those who publically argue what perhaps many privately believe—that this academic disparity is really caused by the genetic differences in human beings. Though it goes against the American value that "all men are created equal," science, history, and experience show that not to be the case. There is a limit, they claim, to how equal we can really expect academic achievement to be.

These are the major explanations offered for understanding the problem of the achievement gap. So before we can speculate on solutions we must examine some of the above theories. Do they accurately define the problem? If so, what are the possible answers to solving the problem? On the other hand if these theories do not accurately define the problem, why not? And what is the real problem that faces our schools and our country?

CHAPTER III

IS THE ACHIEVEMENT GAP THE RESULT OF SCHOOL FUNDING DISPARITIES?

I n the search for solutions to the achievement gap between black and white students, the first task is to define the problem we are attempting to understand and resolve. An obvious candidate for the root of the problem is money. Is the problem that the schools today that have primarily African-American enrollments receive less funding for those schools, which then impacts the quality of education and creates an achievement gap? Would a substantial infusion of additional funds eventually narrow or close the achievement gap?

Opinions of researchers on this subject differ widely. Perhaps the most widely known of the scholars who have investigated this topic is Eric Hanushek who has reviewed and analyzed more than sixty independent works of other scholars addressing this same topic. Hanushek concludes, "Detailed research spanning two decades and observed performance in many different educational settings provide strong and consistent evidence that expenditures are not systematically related to student achievement." Other researchers such as Rob Greenwald, Larry Hedges, and Richard Laine have come to an exact opposite conclusion. They state that their findings show "that school resources are systematically related to student achievement, and those relations are large [and] educationally important."

Since the United States Constitution makes no mention whatsoever of the topic of education, the task of educating and supporting education is left to the states. Even at the state level, traditional practice has been to provide state oversight but assign financing and control mostly to local school districts. Over the past eight or nine decades the balance of who funds education has shifted in most states. In 1920, for example, 80 percent of revenues for public school operations came from county and local taxes. By 1950 that local percentage had declined to 57 percent, and by 1996 it had fallen to 43 percent. Today many, but not all, state governments provide about 50 percent of the funds for public school expenditures. The amount of money coming from the federal government for specific items has always been relatively small, but even that has increased from about 2 percent in 1940 to about 8 percent in the year 2000.

One reason for the increase in the percentage of state and federal dollars has been the growing awareness of the inequalities in per-pupil spending across school districts even within a single state. Another result of these inequities has been constant attempts through the judicial and legislative processes to allocate resources in a more equitable manner. These efforts have been driven, by implication, by the idea that equalizing resources will equalize student educational outcomes. In 1971, in the California Supreme Court case of *Serrano v. Priest,* the court ruled that wealth disparities between school districts resulting in school expenditure differentials were unconstitutional. Two years later, the U.S. Supreme Court, in the case of *San Antonio Independent School District v. Rodriguez,* reaffirmed the right of localities to control their schools, stating that "each locality is free to tailor local programs to local needs." The Court recognized the right to unequal school expenditures. The Court found that "education is not among the rights afforded explicit or implicit protection under the Constitution." This decision, however, has not deterred efforts to challenge nequalities in school spending and local control of education. Challenges to the system have been made in every state of our nation.

Inequalities in school funding have a long history

in our nation, and the practice continues in our own time. In the first decades of the twentieth century white schools in the South got three dollars or more to one dollar for every black child in school. Mississippi spent $52.01 per white child and $7.36 per black child, Louisiana $77.11 per white child and $20.49 per black child. In the 1940s the disparities in school funding in the nation ranged from a low of $100.00 per child to a high of $6,000 per child. The largest funding differences were between spending for white and black children, with the median expenditure for black children being $477.00 while white children were funded at a rate of $1,166.00 per pupil. By the 1960s per-pupil expenditures in wealthy suburban districts were more than twice the amount spent in urban, big-city high schools.

These spending gaps continue today. Thirty-six states have a funding gap between school districts, with a nationwide disparity between high and low poverty differences of $1,348.00 per student. A quick visit to two districts in Illinois illustrates these spending differences in stark ways. Standing out as an exception to the national trend of states' funding 50 percent of school expenditures, in Illinois the state share has fallen to about 27.5 percent from a high in the 1970s of 48 percent. Thus, in Illinois schools are more than ever dependent on the financial wealth and tax-raising capacity of local school districts in which given schools are located. If there is a state where it really matters where children reside in relation to how much money their school receives to educate them, it clearly is Illinois. In Illinois the average shortfall between districts is about $2,465.00 per pupil, although between many individual districts it is substantially larger. That average shortfall number means that for a single class of twenty-five students, the annual amount of that shortfall is $61,625.00 and for an elementary school of four hundred students, the amount the school is not receiving is almost $1,000,000.00.

A short drive north from Chicago, takes one through the tree-lined suburbs of Evanston, Winnetka, Wilmette, and Kenilworth. The winding path of Sheridan Road runs past neatly kept lawns maintained by lawn services and past large and elegant homes where a million dollar home price tag would put the owner at the lower range of home costs. The Kenilworth school district is 93 percent white with 0 percent black population. The average teacher salary is about $74,000. The community has 0 percent low-income residents and spends between $10,000 and $12,000 per pupil in their schools.

About three hundred miles to the south in Illinois, one enters a different world in East St. Louis. Stores are closed or boarded up, and whereas in Kenilworth one sees no litter on the lawns or on the streets, in East St. Louis such a scene is common. The city is 99 percent black. The school district has a low-income population of 96 percent. Teachers' average salaries are less than those in Kenilworth, but certainly it would be hard to argue that they are drastically underpaid. The average expenditure per pupil is $7,700.00 per pupil. The question is, do these different numbers really make any difference in the education students receive, or are other factors more important? Kenilworth exceeds the state academic standards in every category, East St. Louis in none. But is this because of money? Kenilworth is certainly spending considerably more than the state average, but East. St. Louis is spending the average amount of all school districts in Illinois and cannot be said to be grossly underfunded.

The fact is that while there are still wide disparities between states and districts within those states in regard to per pupil spending, the years since 1945 have witnessed a dramatic increase in school funding to a point that today the U.S. commitment to education is among the highest in the world. In inflated adjusted dollars, U.S. education spending has increased from $1,214.00 per child in 1945 to $8,745.00 in 2002. In 1949-1950 the total expenditure for elementary and secondary education was 2.3 percent of GDP, and by the year 2000 that had risen to 4.3 percent of GDP. A United Nation's study actually reported a higher number, showing U.S. spending to be 6.8 percent of GDP. Since the 1960s school funding in the nation has increased by more than 120 percent, and class sizes have fallen from a ratio of one teacher for every twenty-five students to today's figure of one teacher for every seventeen students. In addition, the federal money coming to school districts through the Head Start Program and Title I of the Elementary and Secondary School Act (ESEA) has resulted in nearly eliminating the previous great disparities in educational funding between richer and poorer districts. If, then, the U.S. has tripled the amount of educational spending over the past three decades, what returns have we received on that investment, and, especially, what impact has that massive infusion of money had on narrowing or closing the achievement gap?

Unfortunately the answer to that question is: very little. On the basis of test scores, there appears to be, at best, a minimal relationship between money spent by school districts and how well students achieve academically. An analysis of forty-five separate studies of the relationship between school expenditures and student achievement between 1928 and 1980 came to the same conclusion, and, in fact, identified a decline in that relationship over several decades. In other words, it was found that while more money was spent, achievement levels stagnated and even declined. This is really not a new finding. James Coleman, in his research fifty years ago on equal educational opportunity, found that average per-pupil expenditures accounted for even less than 1 percent in pupil differences in educational achievement.

Some current examples can illustrate the validity of this disconnect between money and achievement. In Shaker Heights, Ohio, an affluent suburb of Cleveland, educational spending is $10,000 per pupil, which exceeds national averages, and black students represent about one-half of the student population. Yet with this large amount of money meant to benefit all students, black students represent 82 percent of the students who are academically failing. The difference in the SAT scores between black and white students is larger than the black-white national score differences on that same test. In the 1999-2000 school year only 4 percent of black students passed Ohio's state test with honors. That is the exact same percentage of black students who passed with honors but attended school in poor districts that had a reputation of having bad schools. One is forced to ask what difference did substantially more money make in Shaker Heights?

In Kansas City, Missouri, by court order, the school district was spending an additional 1.3 Billion (with a capital B) dollars in education and another 2 Billion (another capital B) dollars to upgrade facilities. The results? Dropout rates increased, and standardized test scores went down. Two areas with the highest school expenditures, Washington D.C. and New York City, ranked, respectively, forty-first and twentieth in eighth-grade math on the National Assessment of Educational Progress (NAEP).

Minnesota, Iowa, North Dakota—each of which has among the nation's lowest per-pupil expenditures—all tied for first place in that same NAEP test. Iowa, in fact, which ranks thirty-second in per pupil spending, had the top performing schools in the United States. Minnesota ranked fourteenth in spending but is second in achievement; Wisconsin is ninth in spending and third in achievement. Washington D.C. spends more than $13,000 per student yet ranks among the worst in the nation in student academic achievement. The state of Utah has one of the lowest per-pupil expenditures in the nation yet ranks third in the nation on the percentage of high school students who score at the level necessary in advanced placement classes to receive college credit. When large amounts of money have been directed to school districts with large minority populations, the results have been negligible. Title I has spent 130 Billion (another capital B) dollars over the past thirty years to close the achievement gap with almost no results to show for the large amount of money spent.

All the above examples are not to be interpreted as an argument that schools should not get adequate funding to educate all children or that we should not continue to work toward minimizing the disparity of funding between districts within a given state. Schools must be adequately funded and disparities eliminated. But the numbers cited do call into question whether money is the key missing ingredient to solving the achievement gap. Rather, is money currently being used wisely and in accordance with what we know about effective teaching and learning? Over the past fifty years there has been a change in how money for schools is spent. The proportion of funds that went to teacher's salaries was 60 percent in 1950 and has now dropped to 40 percent. Costs of administration and student special services have taken up those dollars that had previously gone to teachers. But even if we could dramatically increase teacher's salaries, would that alone make a significant impact on putting better teachers in low achieving minority schools and closing the achievement gap? If we could, theoretically, pay those teachers $100,000 per year, would we recruit the highest caliber of our college graduates, and would that salary alone make the difference in closing the achievement gap? Of course, we will probably never in our lifetime have any real answer to that question, but current research on teacher compensation and student achievement may give us reason to doubt widespread success even if that unlikely situation were to occur. A study that explored the relationship between increased teacher compensation and student achievement found that in reviewing all the various research, 78 percent of the studies found that teacher's salaries had no impact on student performance.

But what if, in the spirit of the democratic-capitalist consumer culture in which we live, we chose to invest money in another way, not by giving money to school districts but, rather, to the students themselves? What if we paid students to study and do well on the high stakes tests by which all schools and students are judged today? Could we provide incentive to black students to do better on assessments if we rewarded them with money? After all, if these young people come from low-income or poverty communities, money might be important, and the cash could help the entire family. Michael Sandel, a professor of government at Harvard University, explored those very questions in his book *What Money Can't Buy: The Moral Limits of Markets*. Sandel cites the following examples of some attempts in urban schools to raise achievement by rewarding students with money:

1. New York City paid fourth graders $25.00 to score well on standard tests.
2. In Washington D.C. an attempt was made to reward good behavior. Students could earn money for doing homework, behaving well in school, and maintaining good school attendance. A student could potentially make up to $100.00 every two weeks.
3. Chicago chose to reward higher grades, offering $50.00 for an A, $35.00 for a B, and $20.00 for a C. The top student could receive $1,875.00 for the entire year.

4. The Dallas school district pays second graders $2.00 for every book they read. They must take a quiz to verify that they have actually read the book.

Did these efforts pay off in terms of student achievement? New York found that paying for good test scores did nothing to raise those scores. Chicago's cash for good grades resulted in no improvement on standardized tests. Washington D.C. saw slightly better results in motivating students with behavior problems to get better reading scores. Dallas's effort to reward young children to read more books was the most successful effort.

A dozen states now have programs that offer financial incentives from $100 to $500 to students and teachers for high achievement on advanced placement tests. What was interesting in an evaluation of these efforts was that the student results were no better when the reward was $500 than when the reward was $100. Aside from the issue of the ethical aspect of such programs—some call them bribes—it is clear once again that such strategies for spending educational money will do little or nothing to close the achievement gap in the nation.

The overall conclusion of using various schemes for spending money to increase achievement is that the continuous infusion of greater and greater amounts of money will have a minimal effect on school achievement and on closing the achievement gap. This certainly does not mean that we should refuse additional funds for schools or reduce any amounts. It does mean we need to look more carefully at how, when, where, and why we are spending the money we have.

Clearly, something more than lack of resources is the problem in defining the cause of the black-white achievement gap. In making the case for additional funding for low-income districts, one advocate has said, "High school students living in low-income families dropped out of school [at] six times the rate of their peers from high income families." That statistic may be true, but is it because the school district didn't have adequate funds? Or was it because of something that had nothing to do with school resources? Was the real cause of black underachievement the condition of poverty that characterizes so many of these low-achieving students?

CHAPTER IV

IS POVERTY THE CAUSE OF THE ACHIEVEMENT GAP?

I f there is one aspect of the discussion of the underlying causes of the black-white achievement gap upon which there is little disagreement, it is that children born in poverty environments do not do as well in school as those who are not poor. In order to fully understand the depth or preeminence of poverty as the major cause of black-white educational disparity, a number of further questions must be explored. What percentage of African-Americans is living in poverty environments today? How can we explain the persistence of poverty in our inner-city black communities? What are the multiple implications and results for children who do live in poverty? And, we must ask, are there exceptions to the connection between poverty and poor academic achievement? Finally, if there are exceptions to the connection between poverty and poor school performance, what do these exceptions require us to think about as we attempt to zero in on the real causes of the academic achievement gap?

Poverty in America continues to be a serious problem. For some, such as elderly Americans, we have made substantial progress in ensuring that they can live out their senior years with dignity and relative freedom from economic concerns. Yet for children in America, it is a different story. The United States of America has the highest percentage of children living in poverty of all the twenty-six nations we consider the developed countries of the world. Even with such a troubling statistic, it is important to note that the nation has made progress in reducing black poverty. The percentage of black families who had incomes below the designated poverty line fell drastically between 1940 and 1960, from 87 percent to 47 percent. It is equally important to recognize that this substantial reduction in the poverty rate came primarily before the Civil Rights Act of 1964, before the Voting Rights Act of 1965, and before any affirmative action initiatives in the 1970s. In that same time period the number of blacks moving into white collar occupations, managerial positions, and administrative jobs combined to double the total number of black professionals. The black poverty rates continued to decline in the 1960s from 47 percent to 30 percent and then from 30 percent to 29 percent n the decade between 1970 and 1980. Beginning in the 1950s, however, black male participation in the labor force began to decline. From 1954 to 1965, the black reduction in the labor force was 17 percent, which was larger for African-Americans than for whites during those same years. From 1965 to 1976, black reduction in labor force participation was 271 percent greater than that of whites. Between 1974 and 1984, one-half of black workers in the Great Lakes region who were employed in manufacturing lost their jobs. By the mid-1980s the contrasts between the percentages of black men employed in 1930 during the Great Depression and those employed in 1980 were striking. In 1930 80 percent of black men found some kind of employment, while in 1983 only 56 percent of black men had jobs. Much of this decline, as some but not all scholars believe, was the result of growing technological advances and the transformation of the nation's economy from an industrial base to one increasingly becoming a knowledge, service, information economy that was also becoming increasingly global in scope.

As we have recounted in Chapter II of this book, African-American students had never done well academically, but the lack of school success had been overcome by the availability of low skill manufacturing jobs, which, for the most part, valued physical ability and endurance over formal education, advanced skills, or technical training. From the 1970s on, all that was changing, and these poorly-educated or school dropout black males were out of work and out of viable options. In the black urban ghettos of our major cities, where one of three black men were high school dropouts, the unemployment numbers rose to crisis proportions. Because they were poorly educated and lacked the requisite skills for a new emerging economy, black men were unable to fill the positions these new jobs required. It is also important to recall that our urban centers experienced a mass migration of southern blacks to places such as Detroit, Chicago, New York, Philadelphia, and other urban centers. These migrants had received either a poor education or virtually no education in the South and, thus, were especially vulnerable to the profound economic transformation the nation was experiencing. By the end of the nineteenth century more than 400,000 blacks had left the South; that migration continued for decades. Between 1910 and 1930, Chicago's black population increased from 44,000 to 234,000, in New York City from 100,000 to 328,000, and in Philadelphia from 84,000 to 220,000. During the World War II years, northern cities continued their magnetic pull as multiple job opportunities became available to sustain the war effort. But, of course, at war's end those jobs mostly disappeared.

Now, however, the new economy was creating a new kind of poverty in the black community, which was populated by individuals who were unprepared for the new job requirements. Poverty itself was not new, of course, but the nature of people's responses to poverty and the consequences of that poverty now seemed to be different. In Chicago, for example, in the 1920s only about 8 or 9 percent of poor people, black and white, were dependent for survival on some kind of charity. By the 1980s the War on Poverty championed by President Lyndon Johnson had created a whole series of safety nets and welfare support systems to assist those in poverty. For some, the incentive to find some kind of work, even if work could be found, was diminished. From the 1980s to the end of the century, black poverty increased from the relatively low levels prior to 1960 to a new period of widespread joblessness and dependency on welfare. By the end of the twentieth century the percentage of single-parent black families had risen dramatically, and the majority of those families were living in poverty conditions. In dramatic contrast, four out of five black families that included a husband and wife did not live in poverty. As we progressed into the twenty-first century, the poverty rate among black husband-wife families was below 10 percent. By the year 2000 there were essentially two black Americas. One, in which the majority of African-Americans lived, was the more educated middle- and upper-class black America. The other black America lived in poverty, now classified by an unfortunate new term that entered the American vocabulary: the underclass. This underclass was variously estimated to consist of a low of 3 percent of the poor to a somewhat unlikely high of 38 percent of urban poor. The underclass blacks were those who had been left behind to live in the urban ghettos; the lives of this small percentage of African-Americans continue to have a major impact on both school and society. Since the 1970s a majority of the underclass black families have lived in poverty communities for consecutive generations, compared to only 7 percent of poor white families.

More than 70 percent of black children who are raised in poverty today will continue to live in poverty as adults. Some of the very positive results of the Civil Rights movement have, ironically, been negative for these underclass citizens. Those who were able to become upwardly mobile understandably sought a better life and better home in what they considered a better community. Often these were African-American small-business owners, teachers, postal workers, police and firemen, doctors, lawyers, accountants, and professors. They had jobs, were making a decent income, and could afford to move, and they did because now there were more communities open to them because previous racial restrictions for housing had fallen.

The poor could not make such moves. Many were poorly educated people, large numbers were female single parents, and most had no job or car and no capacity to take those upwardly mobile options. The result was the formation of increasingly isolated black communities populated by similar kinds of individuals—undereducated, unemployed, and unmarried males and undereducated, poor single mothers with one or more children who had few employable skills and were heavily dependent on government assistance for day-to-day living. Gone now were black professional people. Gone now were role models whom young children would see on the streets. And gone were the black business owners. In place of all these people who had left were gang-bangers, drug dealers, and dozens of idle men occupying street corners. Safe streets were a memory of past days. Crime became rampant as did violence and senseless black-on-black killings. Cautious mothers now hesitated to let their children play outdoors, and the journey from home to school made children wary of crossing gang turf and possibly being caught in the line of gunfire.

In a single weekend, Chicago newspapers reported that there were twenty-six shootings in inner-city neighborhoods, fourteen of which were gang-related. On another weekend, these same newspapers reported fifty-two shootings and ten people killed. In 2011 in Chicago there were 588 shootings and sixty-eight killings of young people between the ages of thirteen and eighteen. An overwhelming majority of these tragedies were located in predominantly black south and west sides of the city. These are the conditions in which students come to school. That there are other things on their minds besides history, science, and state testing should come as no surprise.

The consequences of living in poverty and its impact on student achievement are many. The lack of adequate income results in poor health conditions since eating habits tend to favor cheaper, less healthy foods; doctor visits are less frequent because of the lack of medical insurance. The formation of two-parent families becomes almost obsolete as black men are unemployed, and black women see no attraction in marrying a man who cannot find work or will not work. University of Chicago researchers have found that employed black men in the inner city were two and a half times more likely to marry the mothers of their child than were unemployed men. Thus, in today's black underclass communities, between 65 percent and 85 percent of children are born to unwed women who are adolescents or even younger. A study by the Annie E. Casey Foundation found that children who live in poverty and read below grade level by third grade are three times as likely not to complete high school as opposed to children who have never been poor.

The impact of poverty is particularly severe on black boys, who show steady academic decline on the Iowa Achievement Test from third to seventh grades. Too often these poor children attend schools that have a physical environment that resembles prisons more than schools. In urban schools nationally 16 percent have bars on the windows to prevent vandalism and theft. Forty-five percent of the schools employ security guards, 13 percent have metal detectors, and some schools have regularly assigned uniformed policemen on the premises. Security cameras are common at these schools, and almost 37 percent of urban schools fence off the entire school to create what they hope will be islands of safety. School parking lots are routinely monitored. New York City's budget for school security measures topped more than $221 million dollars, and the city's school security personnel now constitute the fifth largest police force in America.

School dropouts in these underclass neighborhoods stand at 50 percent to 70 percent, and for these young people few jobs are available, which makes the unemployment rate among ghetto youth reach 50 percent or more. Among black high school dropouts, the risk of eventual imprisonment now stands at 60 percent. Young blacks today murder each other at a rate nine times the rate of white youth, and estimates are that approximately 30 percent of young black males between the ages of sixteen and thirty-four living in these poverty neighborhoods are ex-offenders. Blacks today constitute about 11 percent of the U.S. population but make up 50 percent of prison inmates. What is also clear is that the response of poor blacks to their poverty environment has become worse in the past eighty years. In 1930 blacks constituted about 22 percent of all prison inmates, a figure that grew to 29.7 percent in 1950, increased again in 1970 to 36 percent, and reached 46.3 percent in 2000.

The purpose of reviewing these tragic and depressing statistics of the conditions of black inner-city life is simply to underscore that the everyday routine most other Americans experience—getting up each morning, eating a decent breakfast, putting on clean and relatively new clothing, walking safely to a school and coming home to a snack and a good dinner, and then asking one's parents for homework help—is a scenario essentially no child in these communities experiences.

So poverty is, without a doubt, a very large contributor to black academic underachievement, but how central to the problem is it? Some other examples require us to pause and think again about whether or not poverty, in itself, is the cause of the black-white achievement gap. For example, in white and black families whose incomes are similar, poor white students perform academically better than poor black students, and middle-class whites perform better than middle-class blacks. On the National Assessment of Educational Progress, poor white boys eligible for free lunch not only performed as well in math and reading as black boys from middle-class families but also better than black boys from affluent families. If poverty is the central cause of the achievement gap, how can we explain the fact that black students do so poorly in non-poverty communities, such as Shaker Heights, Ohio, and Oak Park and Evanston, Illinois, which are upper middle-class and even affluent areas? Something aside from poverty issues is obviously operational in these communities. And then there is the well-documented academic achievement of Vietnamese "boat people" and other poor Asian students. These boat people, mostly Vietnamese but also Chinese and Laotians, came to the United States in the late 1970s as exceptionally poor refugees who had virtually no material possessions. Their families had been broken up; none could read, write, or speak the English language; and the overwhelming majority were uneducated. These enormous obstacles did not seem to prevent the children of this group from succeeding in school. In California they achieved an overall grade point average of B with about half of them averaging an A in math classes. Only 6.3 percent received a grade of D or lower. These students performed equally well in California's so-called bad schools as they did in schools with good reputations. In one county they represented 20 percent of the school enrollment but produced twelve of fourteen valedictorians. Even though poverty rates among Chinese, Koreans, and Vietnamese are higher than among whites, students of Chinese ancestry outnumber black students at the University of California at Berkeley by a rate of five to one.

Another perspective regarding the centrality of poverty in explaining the black-white achievement gap is to be seen by looking at the record of American blacks who were born, or whose parents were born, in the Caribbean. Although this group has not been in a state of poverty at the rate of those defined as the underclass, they are by no means affluent or even primarily in the middle class. Yet these black students are two times as likely as native born blacks to attend the top twenty or twenty-five universities in the United States. In Ivy League universities, native-born African and Caribbean students represent 41 percent of all black freshmen, a hugely disproportionate number considering the small percentage they represent in the overall United States black population. So these examples should make us think again about the relationship between poverty and black underachievement. We cannot forget either the history of white European immigrants to America. They, too, began in poverty, often living in unsatisfactory, overcrowded ghettos and were subject to widespread discrimination. Yet for most, poverty was not an insurmountable obstacle and was not passed on from one generation to the next. By the second generation for many, and by the third generation for virtually every ethnic group, their children were succeeding in school and living normal comfortable middle-class lives.

What then can we conclude about the central importance of poverty in keeping black students from academic success and from matching the level of white students? Probably the safest conclusion is that, yes, poverty is an important reason for the poor achievement of black students, and only those who would ignore or dismiss the facts cited earlier could conclude otherwise. But still, is it the major, central, all-consuming reason? The poor academic performance of black students in every other non-poverty, socio-economic class would lead us to think otherwise. And the normal and high academic performance of other non-African-American students from poverty backgrounds casts even further doubt on a single focus on poverty. The evidence tells us that, if by some miracle, we could instantly eliminate poverty in the African-American community, academic achievement would no doubt improve, but the achievement gap would most likely still exist. So if we cannot settle on poverty as the main cause of the problem we are exploring, where can we now go to seek answers?

CHAPTER V

IS AMERICAN RACISM THE REAL CAUSE OF THE ACHIEVEMENT GAP?

From the first European settlements in North America, racism has been the stain on the American story. For more than 200 years, those of African ancestry were kept in bondage and considered less than human. Black families were torn apart, marriages were forbidden, and attempts to give slaves any education were crimes punishable by law. Negro women were not only servants but also sexual objects subject to the desires of white slaveholders and the sons of those slaveholders. Blacks were bought and sold in public markets with the same disregard for personal dignity as was given cows, pigs, and chickens.

The emancipation of blacks and the events in subsequent decades showed clearly that American racist attitudes toward Negroes were not the monopoly of the American South. Jim Crow laws and discriminatory attitudes and policies found fertile ground in the American North as well, and those conditions lasted well past the middle of the twentieth century. We only need to be reminded that in the *Plessy* decision, the United States Supreme Court legalized school segregation at the dawn of the twentieth century, and it took another half century for the Court's *Brown* decision to make segregation by race illegal, even though for another twenty-five years, parts of America found ways to delay or avoid the decision of the Court. Governor George Wallace's defiance of federal authority, as he blocked entrance of black students to the University of Alabama in the 1960s, and the urban riots of African-American communities following the assassination of Dr. Martin Luther King, Jr., reminded the nation that racism was alive and well. President Lyndon Johnson's leadership in passing the Civil Rights Act and the Voting Rights Act put into law rights that had never had to be specified for America's white citizens. As America watched repeated reruns of the video showing the brutal beating of Rodney King by Los Angeles police and the subsequent destructive riots in that city, it was clear that the issue of white-black racism was still with us in the 1990s.

The election of Barack Obama in 2008 seemed to be a historic change as millions watched America's first African-American president take the oath of office on January 20, 2009. As the new president faced unified opposition for his agenda from Republicans and the upstart Tea Party followers, former President Jimmy Carter, when asked why the president encountered so much opposition, quickly and unambiguously responded that a large part of the opposition was because of Obama's race. Whether or not one accepts President Carter's view, to deny that racism has been a strong and consistent aspect of American life is to ignore facts and deny history. So the issue of race and racism must be considered when assessing the reasons for the poor academic performance of so many African-American students.

A review of the black student experience as the decades progressed from 1900 to the 1960s is a story of growing racist attitudes and isolation of African-American communities, schools, and students. It was these attitudes and conditions of isolation that created many of the issues we face today when attempting to raise African-American student achievement levels. The American South, in the years following emancipation and into the twentieth century, had legal sanction to justify racially segregated schools. The South took advantage of that opportunity throughout the region of the old Confederacy. Delaying tactics and the establishment of white private schools continued the racial separation of students even after the outlawing of racially segregated schools in 1954. At the end of the nineteenth century and in the early years of the twentieth century, blacks met a more accepting environment in the nation's large northern urban cities. In many cities, schools were not racially segregated, and there is little evidence that black students were perceived as especially difficult to discipline or to educate, even though most came from homes in which parents were mostly uneducated and some were even illiterate. These students came from essentially the same backgrounds as those thousands of immigrant students who increasingly were filling the city schools. As has been noted earlier, black students actually remained in school longer than their white immigrant classmates, who chose to find jobs as soon as possible.

During this time period America was experiencing two simultaneous mass movements of people from one location to another. Blacks continued to dramatically increase their exodus from the South to the great cities of the North; at the same time, these cities were absorbing a record number of poor white immigrants from southern and eastern Europe. In such a setting, growing competition for jobs and potential conflict were inevitable, as the tragic Chicago race riot of 1919 showed.

Soon a pattern began to emerge: As movement of Negroes increased into the northern cities, segregation and isolation of blacks became more real and visible. So, too, did these same aspects of black urban life affect the schools.

In 1950 white students had been in the majority in the country's largest school systems, except for Washington D.C. By 1968 six of the ten largest school systems in the nation were more than 50 percent minority, and by 1980 all of these school systems were two-thirds minority; some were 75 percent minority. After 1968, primarily because of court orders, racial segregation in schools actually decreased, with the proportion of African-American students enrolled in all black schools falling nationwide from 64 percent to 33 percent from 1968 to 1980. A similar reduction occurred in the percentage of majority black schools attended by African-American students as that number fell from 76 percent to 63 percent in those same years. Thus, residential segregation and isolation, which grew for blacks between 1920 and 1960 and had resulted in more racially segregated schools, decreased in some, but not all, northern American cities.

As we have recounted in Chapter II, few blacks or white immigrant students found urban schools to be particularly hospitable or useful institutions, but growing negative attitudes toward black students did emerge. In the 1920s black students were not viewed particularly as academic underachievers, but their actions and attitudes were being discussed. In the 1930s teachers began to openly talk about black students' being intellectually inferior. One principal said that his black students were "incapable of abstract thought." Blacks, one contemporary said, "shut down their intellectual processes when they are about twelve or fourteen years of age…they cannot grasp the subject." Today's familiar complaints about black discipline were also increasingly voiced. In 1940 the president of a large urban teachers union wrote that disorder and resistance were characteristics of the black underprivileged schools. By the 1950s one can find comments that characterize black students as having "slouching physical posture and heads on desks," which indicated physical "weariness and lack of personal motivation." In 1955 the Chicago Teachers Union began for the first time to gather statistics on physical school violence and attacks. Their report revealed that between 1955 and 1961 more than two-thirds of these incidents of violence had occurred at predominantly black schools. By the 1960s, then, most of the ingredients that today define the crisis of our urban schools and situations regarding black students seemed to be in place. Tensions between blacks and whites had increased, attitudes about black students began to take shape, and, without doubt, racism and racial attitudes had not only not declined but actually increased in many northern cities.

Today it is understandable, but not entirely accurate, for some to claim that racism exists in our school systems and is an underlying cause of the problems African-American students encounter.

Although laws no longer permit the segregation of people by race, urban residential patterns and the affordability of housing often accomplish segregation without the force of law. Black isolation in schools is evident in the enrollment figures of students in some of our largest cities. When one looks at the percentage of students who attend essentially racially segregated schools, it's clear that the numbers tell the story. In Chicago the number is more than 80 percent, in Philadelphia 70 percent, Houston 70 percent, Los Angeles 69 percent, and New York City almost 80 percent. In New York City enrollment at one-half of the city's 1,600 schools is 90 percent black and Hispanic. Yet while these numbers could be seen as a negative, that is not necessarily the case. We hear few, if any, calls for change when schools are 90 percent or 100 percent white. It is assumed that the racial mix of the schools has nothing to do with the capacity and willingness of those students to learn and succeed. Today there are virtually no calls from black leadership to initiate programs that would alter the racial mix of schools so as to increase black student achievement. In fact, for many African-Americans any strategy for enhancing black achievement through racial integration could be viewed as racism in and of itself, implying that black students must be in the same classroom with white students in order to learn and and that they cannot meet academic achievement standards on their own.

But those who claim that deep seated racism continues to infect our schools have other complaints as well. Black students, for example, represent 16 percent of all public school students but constitute 40 percent of those students classified as having some kind of mental or physical disability. This overclassification and identification of black students as special education students has resulted in some schools' having 30 percent to 40 percent of the student body placed in this category whereas many of those students are simply ones who come to school academically behind and require extra help or tutoring. Often the lack of effort and motivation of inner-city black students is the result of their not being able to visualize a future other than what they observe in their neighborhoods, where violence and drugs are commonplace and unemployed residents are visible everywhere.

John Ogbu, in his study of black students in Shaker Heights, Ohio, observed that those students believed that for a black person to have even a chance of competing successfully with whites in the marketplace for the exact same job, he needed to be twice as good as the white applicant. Hiring audits of job applicants in Washington D.C. and Chicago seem to validate the Shaker Heights students' feelings. Among black and white job applicants with similar qualifications, blacks were discriminated against in 20 percent of the cases. Other studies have shown that young black men applying for entry-level jobs were rejected at twice the rate of their white counterparts. Here too, however, one should be cautious about labeling the situation racist. Other surveys of private-sector employers consistently report that too many young black job applicants do not possess even the basic reading, writing, and simple mathematical skills necessary to effectively perform jobs for which they applied. These applicant rejections are not racist, just good business practice.

Students' perceptions of racist attitudes toward them by their teachers also affect their behavior. The Shaker Heights study reported that a major complaint of the African-American students in that affluent community was that their teachers "didn't care" about them. One cannot determine the validity of this feeling, but, whether accurate or not, if the students genuinely felt this, then for all practical purposes, it was, in fact, true, and they responded accordingly. When black, white, and Asian students were asked in a recent survey whether they agreed with the statement, "My teacher supports me and cares about my success in their class," the responses of all three groups provide an interesting contrast of their perceptions of race. Only 20 percent of black males and 28 percent of black females agreed or strongly agreed with the statement. For Asian students the agree/strongly agree percentage was 66 percent for boys and 69 percent for girls. And for white students the percentages in that same category were 54 percent for boys and 71 percent for girls. Among black students 80 percent of black boys and 72 percent of black girls either disagreed or strongly disagreed with the statement. At least three conclusions stand out in this survey. First, whatever their race, boys seem to have some unidentified issues here because in all three races, they, more than girls, felt that teachers were not supportive and caring. Second, if these negative responses of black students are to be interpreted as some manifestation of racism, clearly there was little evidence of that in the responses of Asian students. But third, one cannot ignore the low numbers of black students who did not support the statement. This feeling of not being cared about is easily interpreted by students as disrespect, and feelings of disrespect are the seeds of lack of motivation and troublesome behavior. Race, then, has been and continues to be an issue that undoubtedly impacts black student behavior and achievement.

How much do these racial attitudes really affect black student achievement, though? If racism is the central cause, how do we explain the low achievement of black students going to all-black schools with all-black school administrators in predominantly black communities that have all-black school boards? Where is the racism coming from in these settings? How can we account for the fact that other groups of Americans have experienced long periods of discrimination against them and yet have not only survived but succeeded academically and professionally?

Each generation of immigrants that has come to America has faced open and often violent racism and discrimination. American schoolbooks in the nineteenth century depicted a large number of Irish immigrants as lazy drunkards who had more allegiance to the Roman Catholic pope than to the United States. On the streets these Irish confronted job discrimination and "No Irish Need Apply" signs daily.

The great period of immigration from 1880 to 1924 saw discrimination and racism against European whites reach new heights of bigotry and hatred. Jews were Christ killers and blood suckers, Italians were dirty dagos and gangsters. Signs in Utah, where Greek immigrants had come to work on railroads, were placed in public places announcing, "No Dogs or Greeks Allowed." Poles and Norwegians were the subject of jokes that had at their core the supposed stupidity of both nationalities. Until our own time, major universities had quotas for which ethnic or religious applicants they would admit. Yet each ethnic group ignored or overcame these racist slurs and has become not only full Americans but individuals who have found success in every aspect of the nation's educational, professional, business, sports, and entertainment worlds. Our historical record makes it clear that racism in this country has not been focused exclusively on African-Americans. It is true, as some will quickly point out, that these other groups may have been subjected to racism, but in skin color they were considered white and thus had the chance to move into the American mainstream where those who were non-white could not. It is sometimes forgotten, however, that for many white, Protestant Americans who complained about these newly arrived immigrants, foreigners from eastern and southern Europe were viewed as not being white at all. Of course, in spite of these early racial classifications, European immigrants were, in fact, white, and that did allow them over time to become accepted as mainstream Americans. There were other immigrants who were not white. How did they cope with majority American racist attitudes?

The American Indians, or, more properly, Native Americans; Asians; Hispanics; and South Asians from India and Pakistan come to mind in our own time. Native Americans were, of course, the first to experience American racism, and their story has not ended well. Forced onto reservations and their land taken from them, today they live in communities where they suffer from high unemployment and excessive alcoholism. The only positive action for them has been the granting of licenses in some states to operate casinos, which are producing some needed jobs and revenue. South Asian Indians and Pakistanis are more recent immigrants who have not seemed to be targets of overt racism. Two advantages are keys to their not experiencing some of the racist responses that other previous immigrant groups have encountered. First, they speak English and can easily take advantage of American educational institutions, and second, many of the adult immigrants have higher levels of education than those immigrant groups that preceded them. Yet they are not white, and although there may be some subtle and silent elements of negative feelings against them, those prejudices do not seem to have held them back from becoming entrepreneurs, business people, and professionals or from succeeding in our schools.

The large and fast-growing Hispanic population has presented the nation with an immigrant condition that it has never before experienced. For the first time large numbers of immigrants came to America from a country whose border we share. Never before has it been so easy for a group of non-Americans, that is, noncitizens of the United States, to enter our country. And never before have we received so large an immigrant group that all spoke a language other than English. Whatever negative attitudes Americans have toward Hispanic immigrants are essentially based on a resentment against those who live here illegally and yet reap the benefits of services and institutions that are supported by public tax dollars. Also, this immigrant group seems reluctant to function in the English language and expects to be accommodated in their native Spanish language. Like previous non-English-speaking European groups who came before them, Hispanic students have not done well in our schools. Their high school dropout rates often exceed those of African-American students in urban schools. Yet although they do not do well in school generally, they most often do better than African-American students when measured on state and national assessments. If they are experiencing discrimination or racism, they appear to be gradually overcoming those barriers and are quietly moving into becoming assimilated Americans, although they, too, are people of color.

If any group has experienced levels of racism and discrimination that parallel, to some degree, those experienced by African-Americans, it is Americans of Asian ancestry. In the 1800s segregation laws prevented Japanese and Chinese children in California from attending schools with whites. In other states they were forced to attend segregated schools with black students; those segregation laws were not removed until the 1950s. Chinese workers were forced out of mining jobs and actually expelled from cities such as Seattle and Tacoma. Some Chinese were lynched by white racist mobs. Between 1854 and 1874, they were prohibited from testifying in court against white defendants. Fear of the so-called yellow peril led to the Chinese Exclusion Act of 1882, which cut off access to legal immigration. Other laws prevented Chinese from acquiring United States citizenship. It was not until 1965 that Chinese immigrants were placed in a nondiscriminatory category with other immigrants. In 1913 Japanese were forbidden by law from owning land, and, of course, the ultimate racist act against the Japanese-Americans occurred during WWII when they were rounded up and placed in internment camps.

Sociologist, Gunnar Myrdal, looking at American society, found the prejudice against Asian-Americans to be very intense. He viewed them as a group that could never be assimilated. Today Japanese-Americans are the second largest ethnic group after American Jews in regard to family income, and they have one of the highest rates of intermarriage with white spouses. Chinese-American students score at the top of nearly every state and national educational assessment. Clearly American racism did not prevent Asian-Americans from not only surviving that discrimination but achieving and prospering at the highest levels.

It is also important to recall that when we investigate the causes of black student underachievement, we are not, of course, speaking of all African-Americans. While most, if not all, black Americans may have experienced some form of racism and discrimination, many have successfully overcome those obstacles. Once again it is appropriate to underscore the fact that the majority of African-Americans in

America are now classified as middle class. In 1950 only one of six Negro Americans was categorized as being part of the middle class, but today two-thirds of African-Americans are part of that socioeconomic group. Obviously racism was not an insurmountable barrier for this large group.

Today black college graduates can expect to earn as much, if not more, than white college graduates in the job market. Those with only a high school education or less, as with Americans of all races, face a bleaker future. Even as far back as the early decades of the twentieth century, when discrimination was far more a part of American society than today, black students in selected schools were academically achieving at high levels. A number of predominantly black schools in New Orleans, Atlanta, Baltimore, and Washington D.C. could boast of high academic performance. In the early 1900s, for example, students at the black Dunbar High School in Washington D.C. scored higher on citywide tests than all the other high schools in that city. The experience of blacks from the Caribbean who came to the United States s also a story of not allowing racism to block progress and achievement. These men and women, whose skin color was the same as that of American blacks, have had a notable record of success in business and leadership roles. They represent only 1 percent of the black population, but by 1970 the second generation exceeded native-born Americans in median family income, level of education, and percentage of persons working in the professions.

If all these success stories of all these various groups are part of the American experience, something more than overt racism must be impacting American inner-city black communities. Whatever that something is, it hinders change and does not allow for academic success for the young people who attend school in those urban neighborhoods. If racism was the single key element holding back success, we would expect that when conditions that foster discrimination were absent, those communities and institutions controlled and operated by African-Americans would find greater success. Unfortunately, there are too many examples where this is not the case. Black control of schools in primarily black communities has not resulted in superior schools or high student academic achievement. One need only look at the academic achievement levels of black-majority communities such as Washington D.C.; Gary, Indiana; East St. Louis, Illinois; Newark, New Jersey; or Detroit, Michigan to illustrate that reality.

There is no doubt that American racism and discrimination have impacted African-Americans for more than 400 years. It would be wrong to ignore that part of our history and not acknowledge that it has had a profound and often devastating impact on black American life. However, it is also clear from the evidence and records of people of other nonblack races, different white ethnic origins, and other blacks themselves that this racism is not and has not been an insurmountable barrier for success. Now, some sixty years after the Civil Rights movement in our nation, legal obstacles for African-Americans have been removed. Yet something else is operating in the black inner-city underclass communities that perpetuates low student achievement, high crime, high incarceration rates, large-scale unemployment, and high dropout rates. In 1965, Daniel Patrick Moynihan released a study of the Negro family in which he argued that the key issue in the plight of inner-city blacks was the disintegration of the family structure. Now, fifty years later, can we say that Moynihan was ahead of his time and that he hit upon the key element in our quest to find the root cause of the academic achievement gap?

CHAPTER VI

IS THE STRUCTURE OF THE INNER-CITY BLACK FAMILY THE CAUSE OF THE ACHIEVEMENT GAP?

In the short two year period of 1965 through 1966, two reports were released that were immediately controversial and continue to have relevance today. The first report, in 1965, was written by a little-known sociologist who was working as an assistant secretary in the United States Department of Labor, Daniel Patrick Moynihan. When the report, entitled "The Negro Family: The Case for National Action," was released, Moynihan became instantly well known; he later represented New York in the United States Senate. The report stated that the Negro family had become a "tangle of pathology" and that the condition of black society was the deterioration of the black family. The report further said that black males were unable to function successfully as authority figures because of the matriarchal structure of Negro families.

Moynihan saw the growth of welfare programs as a symptom of the dysfunction of the black family and predicted that without access to employment, Negro men would not be able to support a family, which, in turn, would lead to abandonment of their families and growing divorce rates. These conditions, he wrote, would lead to increases in female-headed households, poverty, and high rates of out-of-wed-lock births. Moynihan wrote to President Lyndon Johnson that the only way to avoid this future sce-nario was development of vocational and educational training and creation of jobs for the black commu-nity. Immediately upon its release, the Moynihan Report created heated debate and controversy. Some contemporary black leaders charged it contained cul-tural bias, was racist, and was based on stereotypes. Others received the information as a tough but re-alistic view that others had been reluctant to discuss but that now had to be addressed. William Ryan, a psychologist, denounced the report in his book, *Blaming the Victim*. The result was the establishment of the two-sided debate that continues to this day. On one side are those, like Ryan, who say that blam-ing the victim is not a solution, and instead societal conditions that have resulted in contemporary black inner-city problems must be addressed. On the other side are those who today echo Moynihan and say that poverty, violence, poor education, and high percentages of out-of-wedlock births in inner-city black neighborhoods are not the result of societal inaction. After all, they argue, the recommendations Moynihan made were, in fact, implemented. For more than fifty years, city, state, and federal governments have spent billions of dollars on welfare, training, education, and jobs programs targeted to African-Americans, yet the situation today in African-American inner-city communities is even worse than when Moynihan's report was issued.

The second report, which was released the following year, was titled "Equality of Educational Opportunity" and was written by a well-known sociologist, James S. Coleman. This report, in addition to Coleman's follow-up writings, also proved to be controversial because of his conclusions regarding what really influenced student achievement. His study, which had more than 150,000 students in his sample, concluded that student family background and the family's socioeconomic status were more significant in student outcomes than factors such as how much money was allocated to schools. Coleman concluded that the schools students attended did make a difference. He based this conclusion on the quality of the teaching staff and that black students would benefit from being in integrated classrooms but only if those classrooms had a majority of white students. Coleman's report was immediately attacked by some who concluded that the report's message was that schools really didn't matter a great deal in a child's education. In fact, the report made no such statement or conclusion. What it did conclude was that students do learn in schools, but he found that schools have a limited capacity to have a positive impact on the rate at which children from different social classes progress. Now, almost fifty years later, the basic conclusions of the Coleman Report have not been undermined. No researchers have been able to attribute fewer than two-thirds of student achievement differences in schools to the family profile and characteristics of the student. The importance of these two historic reports is that they underscore the key role families play in the potential of students to be academically successful. Yet problems, issues, and difficult to explain situations remain in attempts to assess the past and present role the black family has played in the academic achievement of children.

The statement in the Moynihan Report that the black family had become "a tangle of pathology" was a measurement and comparison essentially against middle-class white families of the time. This does not make the conclusion any less valid, but it is instructive to quickly review some elements of black family structure and life from its African origins and through the period of slavery in our own country. Anthropologists have noted differences between European and African conceptions of what elements constitute "family." The European preference for taking male slaves from Africa had created a sex ratio imbalance between those men and women who remained that had encouraged the development of men taking on plural wives. Thus, the concept of monogamy had little meaning in Africa, and having multiple wives caused no negative social stigma. This idea carried over into the slave period in our own history, and slaves having multiple "wives" with whom they had children was not something necessarily unique to the black men's situation in America. The practice of men having children with more than one woman meant that the offspring would inevitably spend more time with the mother and develop a strong attachment to the mother. Thus developed a family structure in which the mother played a prominent and dominant role and created a form of matriarchy among black families.

In Africa a child was rarely in a negative position in society because of how he or she was born. The concept of illegitimacy that Europeans looked down upon presented no negative status to an African unmarried woman who bore a child. The parentage of a child had little or nothing to do with determining the child's position in society. Contrary to European thinking, the key value in West Africa was not marriage but rather producing children. Children in Africa were regarded as testimony to a man's virility, and marriage and parenthood in general were not the key elements associated with the idea of family. Couples often lived together before marriage, and there was little societal value connected with a woman's being a virgin. Often there was no ceremony connected with individuals being married. Even after marriage, the husband continued to live his life in a similar way to what he had done before, Marriage itself was often not easy or possible because of the requirement of the payment of some kind of dowry, which some could not afford, to a prospective husband. There was also no negative connotation associated with being divorced, and it was not regarded as immoral to move on with another marriage partner without getting a divorce. The value of children was so high that Africans did not understand celibacy and, unlike Europeans of the time, did not view sex as sinful or evil. Premarital sex often began with the beginning of puberty and was accepted by society as a normal part of the process of becoming an adult and being initiated into the process of courtship.

In Africa producing a child was important, and there was a distinct idea of who had responsibility to raise that child. As important was what tribe one belonged to and what kinship network one could identify as one's own. African parents protected their children, but the raising of the child was considered the responsibility of the larger kin group. This explains the origin of the African proverb that states, "It takes a village to raise a child." Once again, in our country, the slave pattern of sharing in child-raising was not only the result of how the slave system often divided a mother-father union but also another direct cultural transmission from the African experience.

An obvious question is how could such cultural aspects of African life survive today, more than 400 years after the first black slaves were brought to the American colonies? The answer is that all aspects of African culture did not survive or were changed, forgotten, or reshaped during that long period of years. Nuclear families, common to Europeans, did develop and in places became the norm for blacks as well. However, given the severe separation of races in the United States throughout virtually all of our history and the continued isolation of pockets of black Americans who have lived in inner cities, it is not impossible that certain African traditions, customs, and values represent a cultural survival that continues to this day.

Although the black experience during those long years of captivity under slavery can, in no way, be described as positive, it would be wrong to conclude that slavery was the cause of the destruction of the black family and that we live today with the consequences of that process. There is no question that cruel acts of separating black slave families did occur, but research has shown that the majority of black families remained intact. Slave marriages, of course, were officially forbidden and had no legal status, but men and women who came together formed families that were long lasting. Most children of slaves grew up in two-parent families, with the majority of children having the same mother and father. Studies done after the Civil War further revealed that most black couples in their forties had been together or twenty or more years. Thus slaves in America created families that were improvised structures, drawing on African traditions but adapting to conditions that surrounded them in America. Mothers and grandmothers continued to play dominant roles, and there were extended lineage ties and a child-rearing process whereby all adults looked after all children. Between 1855 and 1880, 70 percent to 90 percent of black households contained two parents, and at least 70 percent of those households would be considered nuclear. In Philadelphia, for example, black male-headed families were more common among free blacks than among any other group. By the end of the century, about 25 percent of black households in northern cities were headed by females, as were 34 percent of those households in southern cities. Something was obviously beginning to happen that, while not yet reaching the percentages of today, was impacting black families.

Although slavery had not destroyed the black family, some scholars believe that the experience of more than 250 years of generations living in such a closed, harmful institution did leave many freed blacks with a negative legacy. The distinguished African-American scholar Thomas Sowell states, "As workers blacks had little sense of personal responsibility under slavery. Lack of initiative, evasion of work, half-done work, unpredictable absenteeism, and abuse of tools and equipment were pervasive under slavery and these patterns did not just suddenly disappear with emancipation." These traits were hardly the ingredients for employment in a growing industrial America or for a stable and economically self-sufficient marriage arrangement. The massive black migration from the South to the northern urban centers furthered the stress placed on black families. Census data reveal that blacks had slightly higher marriage rates than whites for every decade from 1890 to 1940 but much lower rates by 1960. In 1960 about 11 percent of black single women headed households, but by 2000, 65 percent did and 75 percent of young black mothers had never been married.

Economic conditions, coupled with ongoing discrimination practices, contributed to the further destabilization of the black family. In the early part of the twentieth century only about 4 percent of white women with young children worked outside the home, while the figure for black women was 13 percent. Around 1950 the proportion of black households with a parent who worked full-time for the full year was 45 percent and for whites 57 percent. At that same time about 13 percent of fully-employed whites lived in poverty, but 50 percent of blacks did. The economic necessity of both black husband and wife to work in an increasingly unpredictable labor market placed a toll on black marriages and parental involvement in their children's education and in the supervision of those children.

In Chicago by 1933 the black South Side had the highest rate of out-of-wedlock births of any other part of the city, and the school truancy rate was two times that of white students. Residential mobility was also high with 39 percent of families having lived at their current address for one year and 53 percent for less than two years. In one school, 53 percent of the students who began school in September were no longer in that school by the next June. Thus, by the end of the 1950s the signs of today's black family crisis were present and became the impetus for Moynihan to explore what he perceived as a growing and serious problem.

The decades since the 1960s have defined the current situation in urban inner-city African-American communities. Three key events in the 1960s and in subsequent decades have contributed to a further deterioration of black family life in inner-city neighborhoods and, in turn, have contributed to the growing black-white achievement gap.

The first of these was the government's response to negative trends that had been increasing for all

Americans and that the Moynihan Report focused on in the black community: the growing number of people who were living in poverty. In 1964 President Lyndon Johnson announced the Economic Opportunity Act, which became more generally known as the War on Poverty. This legislation had multiple aspects, each targeting some approach to attacking the causes and solutions to poverty in America. Programs such as Head Start attempted to address the educational and social deficiencies of young children who were living in poverty. The Job Corps and other training programs addressed preparation for employment. Work/study programs for university students, Neighborhood Youth Corps, and Vista (Volunteers In Service of America) were focused on working in poor communities. Finally, Community Action Programs (CAPS) sought to involve people in decisions regarding programs that affected people's lives. So the Great Society's War on Poverty was not simply words or promises. The federal government spent millions of dollars in this huge effort to eradicate poverty from America.

As early as 1935, in the midst of the nation's greatest economic depression, President Franklin Delano Roosevelt had warned in his State of the Union address that "continued dependence on relief induces a spiritual and moral disintegration fundamentally destructive to the national fiber." Just giving poor people welfare checks, Roosevelt said, "is to administer a narcotic, a subtle destroyer of the human spirit." At the time of the launching of the War on Poverty, conservative United States Senator Barry Goldwater spoke out against the idea. Goldwater believed that welfare programs destroyed individualism and enlarged government's role in the lives of Americans. Government policies, Goldwater said, "which create dependent citizens inevitably rob a nation and its people of both moral and physical strength." Goldwater further made a connection between huge welfare programs and crime and illegitimate births. When "the have-nots can take from the haves" through taxation, that process, he said, contributes to crime, riots, and to encouraging people to bear children out of wedlock.

The consequences of this massive anti-poverty initiative were unexpected and for the most part negative. Certain trends and traits that were already a part of poor people's lifestyles were now made stronger and more evident, and individuals were given fewer incentives to work and leave the welfare rolls. The increased availability of cash assistance, food stamps, subsidies for housing, and medical and disability insurance gave many who were poor greater incentives to stay on or get on welfare assistance programs. These new poverty assistance programs created a situation in which an individual no longer had to work in order to survive. Holding a job was no longer necessary, and, in fact, working full time in some undesirable entry-level position often resulted, after taxes, in less take-home pay than one could receive through various public Great Society programs. Many laws actually discouraged individuals from being married because one could receive larger benefits by remaining single. Situations were created whereby a single woman with children could receive more financial benefits from government welfare programs than she would if she had a gainfully employed husband. Thus, the incentive was created for a man and woman not to marry, to have a child, to live apart, and to collect welfare payments that both could share in some way. The welfare programs created an incentive for increasing numbers of out-of-wedlock births. The attractiveness of these government benefits also gave people who were marginally poor the incentive to quit work altogether because they could receive more money and live better if they left their low-paying jobs, stayed at home, and qualified to receive government subsidies.

In the immediate short term, the War on Poverty seemed to hold some promise. The number of people on poverty declined from 16 percent in 1968 to 11 percent in 1978. Many of the programs took people off the welfare rolls temporarily, but they soon found themselves back on; more individuals who had not been on assistance found ways to get on the welfare rolls. Between 1978 and 1982 the number of children under six years old increased by 40 percent.

Elderly blacks experienced three times the poverty rate of elderly whites. By 1982 almost half of black children were poor compared to 17 percent of white children. The increase in female single-family households also revealed the failure of the War on Poverty as the number of black female-headed households went from 54 percent for all black persons at the start of the program to 71 percent by 1982. By 1990 75 percent of all black families living below the poverty line were headed by a single woman. From the lowest percentage of Americans living in poverty in 1978 (11.4 percent), the percentage of blacks living in poverty continued to rise, while the percentage of whites in poverty declined. In the beginning years of the twenty-first century, statistics tell a story of a hard-core number in poverty that remains today. About 25 percent of blacks now live in poverty, while about 7.5 percent of whites are in that category. One-quarter of black children live in poverty as opposed to 7 percent of white children, and among female-headed households, about 45 percent of blacks live in poverty compared to 25 percent of whites. Today more than 60 percent of African-American poor people live in the inner cities of major metropolitan areas, thus residing in increasingly isolated and culture reinforcing environments.

A second event that had a profound and often devastating impact on the inner-city African-American community was the fundamental change that was occurring in the American economy. That change was the rise of an increasingly global economy in which the United States was a major, but no longer the only, economic power. Technological and transportation advances were ushering in a new service-, information-, knowledge-based economy leading to the erosion and decline of the manufacturing sector. These revolutionary changes had a profound impact on African-Americans. In the 1960s the black unemployment rate in the country was 10.2 percent; by 1970 it had fallen to 8.2 percent. Then something began to happen. In 1975 black unemployment rose to 14.8 percent and by 1985 had gone to 15 percent. Other numbers painted an increasingly troublesome picture. The number of black, female-headed households continued to increase and reached 54 percent by the year 2000. The racial makeup of our prisons also revealed a dramatic shift. In 1950 the racial make-up of prison inmates was overwhelmingly white—standing at 70 percent for whites to 35 percent for blacks. By 1970 those percentages changed to 61 percent white and 36 percent black; thirty years later the numbers shifted to 36 percent white versus 46 percent black. Today blacks make up the racial majority in our prisons.

The old economy had required only a minimum education—or sometimes none at all—for an individual to find employment. People could work on a manufacturing assembly line or in a steel mill without much formal education. The new, emerging economy, however, was totally different. Now an education was absolutely essential. Skills were needed in literacy, mathematics, computer technology, problem solving, and critical analysis. Increasingly African-Americans, who had been heavily employed in manufacturing, were losing their jobs, and many of the now high-tech manufacturing facilities moved from their inner-city locations to far-out suburbs. As we noted earlier, the gradual elimination of discriminatory barriers regarding housing also had an ironically negative impact on less educated inner-city blacks. Those African-Americans with the education and skills to function in this new economy could now move to many city neighborhoods and suburbs that had previously been off limits to blacks when more rigid discriminatory practices were in place. Left behind in inner-city communities were undereducated, poorer blacks who not only could not afford to move but who could not qualify for new knowledge-, information- and service-based positions. At the very time a good education was becoming the only avenue to economic success in America, schools in inner cities were performing badly and getting worse every year.

This rise in joblessness in inner-city black America resulted in many negative developments. Increasingly these communities were isolated islands of poor, unemployable people. Middle-class black businessmen, lawyers, doctors, accountants, and other professionals moved to other locations, thus depleting these communities of middle-class, employed role models. The lack of jobs made it difficult for married couples to stay together and, for many, even to consider whether they should marry at all. These conditions led to dramatic increases in out-of-wedlock births and an escalation in the number of female-headed households. These female-headed households increased the demands for welfare assistance because there were few or no child care options that would allow these women to secure full-time employment. The overall result of this lack of work and isolation was an increase in welfare dependency, increased community crime, violence, and drug dealing. The removal of the middle class from these neighborhoods eliminated what had been a force for stability. This group had been the school teachers and grocery and dry cleaning owners. Stores were now closed or perhaps operated by immigrant groups, which often fostered new conflicts and antagonisms. These social and economic forces were the root causes of the creation of a black underclass in America.

The third event was the change in family dynamics. This underclass now saw fewer two-parent families and fewer encounters with black professionals or black entrepreneurs. Out-of-wedlock births became the rule rather than the exception. The increase in the number of unemployed black males accounted primarily for the rise in single-parent families.

The result has been that the United States, among all nations, now leads the world in out-of-wedlock births. Among the dominant races the figures are 67 percent for blacks, 41 percent for Mexican-Americans, 23 percent for whites, 8.4 percent for Chinese-Americans, and 9.2 percent for Japanese-Americans. In Chicago's black inner city, only 25 percent of black families with children are those with two parents. For many inner-city black, girls having a child proves their attractiveness to men. The child bestows on them the status of a grown woman, and illegitimacy in the community does not carry any stigma or shame. Sexual activity among teenagers is accepted, and black males often feel peer pressure to be sexually active. There is little pressure to marry, and temporary relationships are more often the rule than permanent commitments. The high percentage of out-of-wedlock births correlates in the black community with levels of education, with better educated black women more likely to marry than those who are uneducated and poor. Overall, of course, changing national attitudes have made having a child while unmarried more acceptable among some Americans. Today 60 percent of Americans say sex between an unmarried man and woman is morally acceptable, and 54 percent say that having a child outside of marriage is also morally acceptable.

All of these historic and contemporary family developments have an impact on the black child's education. Research indicates that an average professional parent speaks more than 2,000 words per hour to their child, a working-class parent averages 1,300 words per hour, and poor parents on welfare speak about 600 words per hour to their child. The result is that by age three the children of professional parents have a vocabulary 50 percent greater than that of working-class children and two to three times the vocabulary of poor children. Children of poor single parents have fewer educational toys, and there are fewer, if any, books in the home. These same poor children seldom engage in any storytelling at home and too often cannot classify objects by shape, color, and size as they enter kindergarten. About 13 percent of white children watch six or more hours of television each day, but 42 percent of black children watch TV for that many hours. Children in the inner city receive many more reprimands than encouragements from their parent; a three–year-old child has heard 75,000 words of encouragement compared to 200,000 words of reprimand. These inner-city families are increasingly mobile, and that mobility impacts the child's education. About 30 percent of poor families attend an average of three schools by the third grade, while only 10 percent of middle-class children have the same experience. Studies have concluded that if the average mobility of black students were reduced to the same level as the mobility of white students, this alone would likely reduce the academic test score gap by about 7 percent.

A study by the National Educational Longitudinal Survey of 25,000 eighth-grade students who were followed through high school investigated the impact of family and neighborhood on student performance and found that family characteristics were thirty-five to 105 more powerful than school input in student academic performance and twelve to twenty-four times more important than the variables associated with the child's neighborhood. These findings underscore the validity of James Coleman's research done some decades earlier. But these findings still do not provide the full explanation for the achievement gap. Some aspects still require further digging.

Anthropologist John Ogbu researched the academic performance of black students in a community far different from an inner-city ghetto: Shaker Heights, Ohio. This was a community of affluent families of various races. The majority of black families were by no means poor but rather middle and upper middle class. Both black parents and their children spoke of the importance of education and of the necessity of high standards. These were not dysfunctional families but rather normal, stable, American families. Yet the academic performance of the black students, who had the same access to the same school and same teachers as the white students, consistently fell short of the performance of the white students.

How could this be? How can we explain this? Don't situations like this and similar ones found in other middle- and upper-class communities in the country run counter to everything Coleman wrote about as well as what we know about the impacts of poverty and racism? Is something more fundamental at the core of this black-white achievement gap? Are the kids of some races just simply smarter than others? Perhaps the answer is in the area that few dare to enter in America—the topic of genetics and achievement.

CHAPTER VII

COULD THE PROBLEM BE IN OUR GENES?

Any discussion of genes and genetics makes Americans immediately uncomfortable. As a multiracial, multiethnic nation peopled by individuals whose geographic origins cover our planet, we are compelled by our values and by necessity to avoid any serious discussion that might offend one group or another or be a cause for conflict between groups. Our basic and deeply held values of equality and democracy also prohibit any extended consideration of the topic of differences between anyone. "All men are created equal" our founding document says, and all are given certain "unalienable rights" that all cherish, such as "life, liberty, and the pursuit of happiness." Yet, of course, we only need to open our eyes to see that, aside from those God given rights, we are in so many ways very unequal. Some of us are tall, others short; some skinny, others fat;

some fair-skinned, others darker; some have brown hair, others red, blond, black, or none at all. Different races have different facial and eye configurations. Some of us grow to adulthood with much body and facial hair, others with little or none at all. Some of us are good at math or writing, others excel in music, art, or science. To note such obvious differences is not to say or imply that any one of us is better than anyone else, only that we differ in many, many ways. Thus to be different does not mean a category of better or worse, only different.

Yet when we attempt to follow the same logic when considering intelligence, we immediately confront problems. In our society it is almost a forbidden topic of open conversation. Today the National Basketball Association is is made up of incredibly talented and athletic men, the overwhelming majority of whom are African-American. Major league baseball has become, in recent years, a sport dominated by talented men of Hispanic origin. These realities are accepted by the American public with little comment or concern. There are no white, brown, or Asian-ancestry citizens conducting marches or sit-ins in protest of the NBA's lack of non-African-Americans in that sport. No demonstrations or boycotts face major league baseball by whites or blacks because of Hispanic domination of that sport. And there are no calls for affirmative action programs to hire players who aren't African-American or Hispanic in order to more appropriately reflect the racial and ethnic makeup of the country. It is accepted that those two sports are the way they are because of the talent, ability, and determination of those players who compete. When the topic is intelligence and achievement, though, the story is very different.

Facts are facts, and we cannot ignore them; however, we must try to understand and explain them. The numbers are troubling. At every socioeconomic level, from the well-off to the poor, white students academically outperform black students. White students continue to outperform black students on the NAEP in every single state where results are reported. In my own state of Illinois, in every single one of the multiracial school districts, white students outperform black students. In most of those same districts, where there is a measurable Asian-American student population, those students outperform both white and black students. These are not random, isolated cases; when such results occur in virtually all categories, some explanation, genetic or otherwise, is called for.

Before we dig more deeply into the situation in our own country, it is useful to gain a perspective from outside our borders to see examples of other groups' academic success. On international tests that rank the top thirty nations in terms of student achievement, there is not a single Latin American, African, or Muslim nation. In Canada Caribbean-born black students are substantially underachieving, yet

African-born blacks have more success and high enrollments in advanced placement classes. Canadian blacks have the highest percentage of students who do not live with both parents as well as the lowest rate of university completion. In England West Indian blacks have very poor academic achievement levels, but they score higher than students of Pakistani origin. In England students of Italian, Greek, Indonesian, and Turkish origins fall academically behind, yet in Germany students of Greek and Spanish origin score above the national average. In Australia Asian- and Greek-origin students have disproportionately high achievement levels when one considers what percentage of the population they represent. In Ireland a traditionally nomadic group known as the Irish Travellers, although of Irish ethnic origin, show consistently poor academic performance. In Europe no group can really be equated with the American underclass, but perhaps the Roma, better known as gypsies, come closest. In the past they were enslaved and persecuted and were victims of the Holocaust; today they still face segregation throughout European schools and have poor academic achievement records. Such a conflicting and confusing picture of the facts presented above can only serve as a note of caution when one attempts to generalize as to the intelligence of any one racial or ethnic group.

Any genetic explanations are further complicated when one looks more closely at Great Britain. In some ways the situation of student underachievement is similar to that found in the United States, but there are differences as well. There are achievement level differences between native English students and immigrants and people of color. Students of Indian origin outperform those of Pakistani background, and, most notably for our inquiry, blacks from Africa perform at higher levels than blacks from the West Indies. In both the above cited instances, one would be hard pressed to conclude that these differences are caused by genetics because in both cases the genetic origins of each group are essentially the same. Across all English social classes, blacks scored lower than whites of that same social class. Interesting to note is that, as we have discussed in a previous chapter, blacks from the Caribbean stand out in the United States by their academic achievement, family stability, low unemployment, and low incarceration rates. If poor intelligence genes are affecting them negatively in Great Britain, those same genes are functioning very well in the United States.

The English Caribbean blacks display many social characteristics that are a part of the urban black American environment. Caribbean women are most likely to have a child with a father who does not live in the home; the percentage of single parents is high. The women are more likely to be employed than men, and 50 percent of Caribbean fathers are unemployed. Employers characterize the black Caribbean population as "relatively unprepared...and have noticeable difficulties in both literacy and numeracy when compared to their white peers." In developments that are similar to those in our schools, these black students are between four to six times as likely to be expelled from school as are other students. The students continue to have many discipline problems that English teachers characterize as "bad attitude," "arrogance," or "insolence," which results in conflicts between teachers and students. Black girls do better than black boys, but overall the students are behind in all age groups; the gap between West Indian students and their peers widens between the ages of eight and fifteen.

Since no European nations have a history of slavery within their borders that compares with ours, the explanation for the underachievement of so many non-native students, but particularly black English students, is most often made in non-historical terms. Generally there is a lack of research and data in most European countries regarding achievement differences between various racial and ethnic groups. Certainly there is nothing similar to our compilation of massive statistics and information that looks from every angle and variable at the academic achievement and progress of these same groups. One would be hard pressed to identify a national goal or crusade to eliminate the achievement gap or even to give a name or label to achievement disparities. Explanations given for these academic differences vary. Europeans generally focus on school and societal structures and inequalities rather than on individual behavior as the cause.

A major study conducted in England concluded that the academic problem of black student school failure is "the underachievement of the system in providing for such students." To others, the poor performance of most of England's immigrant groups is explained by cultural differences, most notably, that some cultures consider schooling to be harmful because it can distance children from their families and introduce them to different cultural values. If there is one theme that seems more prevalent than others in the English approach, it is that the socio-economic position of the parents may be the key factor in explaining achievement differences. One study concluded that in the United Kingdom the relationship between children's educational attainment and the socioeconomic status of their parents is the most important factor. Most ethnic minority groups, another report concluded, have an equal or even slightly better educational opportunity in England than they had in their home country when class origin is taken into account. As was noted earlier, although in England Indian students have high academic achievement scores, they also have the highest proportion of parents in the high socioeconomic class. One commentator explained the inner-city riots that occurred in London in 2011 in words that echo what we would characterize as ghetto behavior of the underclass in America. London's inner-city kids, he said, have isolated themselves into a counterculture of contempt for mainstream society. This black street culture, he wrote, is imported from the United States and is a "nihilistic grievance culture" fanned by parts of the rap scene. This black counterculture, he concluded, had merged with the "rejectionist, anti-education culture of the bottom end of the white working class." It was this combination of values, attitudes, and frustrations that led to social upheaval. Observers who were not caught up in the emotion of the London riots had a more measured view of the black educational condition: In order to reduce educational inequalities for some migrant and minority groups, it is crucial to improve their socioeconomic status. Thus, while there are some differences, one fact remains when we look at black achievement in schools away from our own nation. In each of the examples given, black students continue to underachieve in comparison to their white peers, so the question remains: Could fundamental genetic differences in intelligence be the cause?

In our own country the discussion of the role of genes and intelligence continues to bring forth contradictory results. In their very controversial book *The Bell Curve*, Richard Hernstein and Charles Murray state that even if home and school conditions and environments could be equalized, natural ability will result in some children's academically outperforming others. They go on to say that "hereditary meritocracy" will arise in our schools. Thomas Sowell, in his book *Race and Culture*, points out that black females have higher IQ test scores than black males and suggests that such results among persons of the same race should make us question what, if anything, race has to do with IQ. He further inserts complicating information into the topic by reporting research that has found that among white-raised black orphans, there was no such female IQ advantage over black boys. Sowell's research concludes that neither for minorities nor anyone else is there a correlation between any test scores and future success. But then Christopher Jencks and Phillips in their in-depth statistical study leave the question of the importance of genes unanswered when they conclude that neither socioeconomic differences nor differences between schools are good explanations of why white children outperform black children who initially have similar skills. The conservative Heritage Foundation analysis of the Programme for International Student Assessment (PISA) concluded, "If white American students were counted as a separate group, their PISA reading scores would rank third in the world, while, if Hispanic and black students were also counted as a separate group, they would rank thirty-first and thirty-third, respectively."

Lawrence Steinberg, in his research-based book of high school students *Beyond The Classroom*, could conclude that ethnicity was the most important factor in regard to student academic performance. The example of Jews and Asians is often cited as proof that some kind of genetic factors influencing academic success must be at work. How could it be, these scholars ask, that both of these two groups perform so well academically in relation to so many millions of people in many different countries and cultures in a variety of economic conditions? Their answer is that one cannot automatically dismiss genetic factors. Asian students from homes with low incomes outperform white, black, and Hispanic students from homes that are equally low income, and middle-class Asian students academically outperform middle-class white, black, and Hispanic students as well. Lawrence Steinberg writes that it "is more advantageous to be Asian than to be wealthy, to have non-divorced parents, or to have a mother who is able to stay home full-time." In other words, in Steinberg's view, simply being Asian overcomes those factors that are commonly cited as contributing to poor student performance. Certainly Steinberg is talking about some kind of genetic influence here.

Our nation's history in attempting to measure intelligence through IQ tests can only lead one to be skeptical regarding the validity of such tests to measure intelligence or future success. At times our Eurocentric view of the world makes us forget or ignore the fact that for a long period of time Europe was not the focus of the civilized world; Egypt, China, and other places were also displaying intellect and culture. Thus, if there were such a thing as superior intelligence among Europeans, it certainly did not blossom for a very long time. IQ tests given to American soldiers in the early decades of the twentieth century showed great disparities in regard to various ethnic group intelligence. Of those groups that exceeded national norms, the following ethnic groups had these percentages: English, 67 percent; German, 49 percent; Irish, 20 percent; Russians, 19 percent; Italians, 14 percent; Polish, 12 percent. When Jewish Americans took these tests in the 1920s, they scored at the bottom of the IQ range. These results, one psychologist said, "disprove the popular belief that the Jew is highly intelligent." These same tests showed low IQ scores for Italians, Greeks, Poles, Hispanics, and Slovaks. One wonders what this psychologist would say today when more than one-fourth of all American Nobel Prizes winners have been Jewish, although Jews make up only about 2 percent of the American population. And what would be the response of those administering those tests who concluded that Chinese were poor in dealing with abstractions, yet today Chinese-American students are among the leaders in math and sciences? How, too, would they explain that by 1960 the children of those Greeks who had scored so poorly on IQ tests in the 1920s possessed the highest educational levels of all ethnic groups and were exceeded only by Jewish-Americans in average income? In the next census in 1970, Greek-American men and women were more likely to have completed college than all of the children of the native population and had income levels 32 percent higher than the average native American population.

It is true that the IQ numbers of blacks in the United States have been consistently around 85 compared to the national norm of 100. Yet even here there are reasons to doubt placing too much emphasis on these scores as the explanation for the black-white achievement gap. Black Americans raised in the North have higher IQ scores than those raised in the South, a fact one can hardly attribute to genetics; black orphans raised by white families have IQs at or above the national average. Once again the experience of West Indian blacks in the United States makes one seriously challenge any theories that attribute the academic achievement gap to genes. The West Indian blacks had, as some historians argue, an even harsher slavery experience than American blacks, yet their income today exceeds that of American blacks, and the second generation of this group has higher income levels than American whites. If genes were a key factor in black underachievement, West Indies blacks do not seem to have paid any attention to their genes. Current IQ tests show that black IQ today is now higher than what white IQ was a generation ago. What is clear is that over time these IQ scores change and sometimes change dramatically, while the gene pool for most stays essentially the same.

The much publicized high academic achievement of Asian students also reveals major differences when one looks at various Asian ethnic groups. For example, Chinese, Japanese, Korean, South Asian, and Vietnamese students score better than their white classmates, while Cambodian, Laotian, and Pacific Island students fall behind white students in their school performance. Only 6 percent of Laotian students and 11 percent of Cambodian students reach college-level readiness in school, while 41 percent of Chinese students and 38 percent of Korean students achieve that performance level. Chinese, Korean, and Asian Indian students are among the most educationally successful in our country, with college completion rates of 67 percent, 59 percent, and 76 percent, respectively, in the year 2000. Among all Asian-Americans, the Chinese have the highest academic achievement levels, while Filipino students are among the lowest. So for those who would argue that Asians have superior genes for intellectual pursuits, they might better look at the evidence and probe deeper for more logical and fact-supported explanations.

The historical record of IQ testing shows little evidence of the intellectual superiority of one particular race or ethnic group over another. IQ clearly has changed over generations. From 1947 to today it has gone up by about eighteen points. The IQ difference between black and white twelve-year-olds has narrowed from fifteen points to about nine and one-half points over the past thirty years. We also know that many factors affect IQ scores. Poor prenatal care, hunger, vitamin deficiency, lead poisoning, alcohol and drug poisoning, poor schools, emotional trauma, and excessive mobility all have an influence on IQ. Many of these factors are part of the lives of those African-Americans who are poor and live in inner-city communities. A generation ago James Coleman summarized the significance of tests well, saying, "These tests do not measure intelligence, nor attitudes, nor qualities of character. Furthermore they are not, nor are they intended to be, 'culture free.' Quite the reverse: they are culture bound. What they measure are the skills which are most important in our society for getting a good job and moving to a better one, and for full participation in an increasingly technological world." The detailed study of the black-white achievement gap by Jencks and Phillips concluded that there was no support for any genetic explanation of black-white IQ differences. Their statement warrants extensive quoting:

The studies most directly relevant to the question of whether IQ difference between blacks and whites is genetic in origin show no association between IQ and African as opposed to European ancestry.... In sum the most relevant studies provide no evidence for the genetic superiority of either race, but strong evidence for a substantial environmental contribution to the IQ gap between blacks and whites. Almost equally important, rigorous interventions do affect IQ and cognitive skills at every stage of the life course. Moreover, the IQ difference between blacks and whites in the United States has narrowed in recent decades. The evidence thus indicates that if there are genetically determined IQ differences between the races, they are too small to show up with any regularity in studies covering a wide range of populations and using a wide range of methodologies.

In recent years we have also identified additional aspects to understanding an individual's potential academic and future success. Harvard psychologist Howard Gardner has been the leading spokesman for what he has labeled "Multiple Intelligences." Speaking about IQ tests, Gardner has said, "The whole concept has to be challenged; in fact, it has to be replaced." Gardner and his colleagues, in effect, redefined what intelligence is and put forth a concept stating intelligence is multifaceted and can take at least seven different forms. They identify these as logical-mathematical, spatial, linguistic, bodily-kinesthetic, musical, interpersonal, and intrapersonal. Other researchers have suggested that perhaps there are additional categories as well. Individuals may possess one or more of these intelligences; the results are that some of us learn by reading, others through visual images, others through how we relate to others, still others by musical or artistic means, and some by physical movement and activity. The significance of such a definition of intelligence is that IQ or standardized tests given to students measure only a small segment of these categories, and our teaching-learning processes are based essentially on the logical-mathematical and linguistic categories. This may lead us to believe that large numbers of students who are classified as not being intelligent may, in fact, be potential learners in one of the seven other intelligences categories. Many of these students would, most likely, not do well on standardized tests that are currently in use.

A second development has been the identification of EQ, or emotional intelligence, as a key factor in predicting an individual's potential for success. As we have seen from the discussion of IQ in the above paragraphs, the actual cause and effect of IQ and success has a muddled and contradictory history. EQ has in recent years been added to our understanding of the definition of intelligence. Whereas intelligence has been generally defined in terms of mental or cognitive ability, advocates of EQ argue that the ability to relate interpersonally is another type of intelligence. This entails the ability to interact with others. Individuals with high EQs are said to be in touch with their emotions and possess the ability to control their feelings. They can control anger, stay focused, and remain balanced. They can read and relate to others' emotions as well and have a sense of empathy that allows them to put themselves in the place of others for better understanding. They are also able to engage in conflict resolution and negotiate issues of dispute. This dimension of intelligence, clearly important to an individual's future success, is also not measured by IQ or any other standardized test that measures student abilities or potential success in college or the workplace,

Understanding, defining, and measuring intelligence is then a complicated process. Using IQ tests, past and present, to identify fundamental causes of the black-white achievement gap is clearly inadequate and incomplete. The evidence is clear: We cannot look to genetics to understand the causes of the black-white academic achievement gap. What then is left for us to explore? If money, poverty, racism, family, and genetics offer no definitive answers, what, if anything, does?

CHAPTER VIII

IS CULTURE THE REAL CAUSE OF THE ACHIEVEMENT GAP?

The American novelist F. Scott Fitzgerald is said to have remarked to Ernest Hemingway, "You know the rich are different from you and me." Hemingway's short reply was, "Yes, they've got more money." In our own day liberal activists have made the same point in a different way saying, "The only difference between the poor and the rest of us is that they have less money." Our American democratic values want both of those observations to be true, but are they really?

Some short snapshot views might help us clarify the issue. When John F. Kennedy was a Senator he was said to carry little or no money with him. In a life where others were around to take care of his needs or pay his bills, the need to worry about whether or not he left the house with some cash was not a daily issue of stress. During the 2012 Republican primary election campaign, Mitt Romney, in a televised debate, challenged his opponent, Texas Governor Rick Perry, to a $10,000 bet to show that one of Perry's accusations against Romney was untrue. Romney casually threw out the figure of $10,000 in the same way most people might say, "I'll bet you a dollar," on some issue of contention. To a man of Romney's wealth and upbringing, $10,000 was not an overly large sum of money to wager on anything. Or, in another nonfinancial snapshot, take a walk on many of the select prestigious university campuses in our country, and you will be struck by what appears to be an inordinately large number of Asian-American students and an almost invisible number of African-American students. Today Asian students outnumber blacks at seven of eight Ivy League colleges, and Asian students today make up more than 20 percent of the student body at more than a dozen U.S. colleges. In still another different setting, listen to the Jewish comedian who tells the following story: "A Jewish mother is walking down the street with her two sons. A passerby asks her how old the boys are. 'The doctor is three,' the mother answers, 'and the lawyer is two.'" Such humor brings a smile to our face because it rings so true. How many other ethnic groups could use that same joke and get a similar response? Not many. Let's take one final walk on the streets of Chicago's West Side, or Gary, Indiana, or in the neighborhood of the Stewart school in Detroit.

One thing that will immediately catch our eye will be broken windows, boarded up houses and storefronts, and many streets and lawns littered with paper, cups, and other items. Walk less than two miles from that Chicago West side neighborhood into the integrated suburb of Oak Park, Illinois, and we will observe none of the broken windows, boarded structures, or litter on the streets.

There must be a reason for each of the above scenarios—if, in fact, the difference between being rich or middle class or poor is only a matter of money, and except for that money we are really all the same, then how can we account for such differences? Certainly we are all equal in the eyes of God and under our national Constitution. And common sense tells us that it is not that some people are good or better and others are not good or worse as human beings because of the money they have or the location of their residence. But clearly something is different. The explanation that makes the most sense to many, but offends many others, is the idea that there are, in fact, definite cultural characteristics among different social classes and that there is something that can be defined as a "culture of poverty."

Those who reject the concept claim it is merely a way of blaming poor people for bad behavior, and this ignores societal forces such as racism, history, and ongoing discrimination. Those who accept the idea that a culture of poverty exists see it only as a subset of overall American culture, which includes a culture of the rich, a culture of the middle class, and a culture of those who are poor. This is not to ascribe superiority or inferiority to any one over the other; it is simply a statement of observable fact. But, say those who acknowledge these variations of American cultures, in order to be successful and socially and economically mobile in America, individuals need to accept, internalize, and act according to American middle-class culture. This was the lesson learned and the path followed by every foreign ethnic group before it could become included into the American mainstream and become socially and economically mobile and successful.

Ruby Payne, in her book *A Framework for Understanding Poverty*, presents the chart on pages 132–133 that she calls the "Hidden Rules Among Classes."

It is important to stress that neither Payne nor anyone else is saying that the traits of the poor she identifies are universally common to all poor people of any race. She is particularly speaking of what is called generational poverty, which speaks to those traits, values, and actions that develop when individuals and their offspring are in a state of poverty and residentially isolated for two to three successive generations. She is not speaking of what has been called situational poverty, which occurs when an individual through illness, job layoffs, or external economic conditions beyond the person's control experiences joblessness and loss of income that place the individual in a poverty condition for some shorter period of time.

One need not accept all of Payne's analyses at face value, but any of us who have worked in poverty neighborhoods and schools know much of it rings very true. In many inner-city schools, students are chronically late or absent, children are not picked up after school, and discipline problems are excessive. A parent may refuse to pay for a school field trip but will readily pay in excess of 100 dollars for a pair of designer gym shoes their child wants. In one Chicago school, coats donated for her children to wear during the city's cold winters were sold for money to purchase drugs for the mother. Students will often refuse to take teacher direction and respond with obscenities, and when they are told that such language is inappropriate, they answer that it is, in fact, appropriate since they report those words are used regularly in their homes. Obviously, such examples are not universal, but they are real and more widespread than we would like to believe. But are they manifestations of a culture of poverty?

One way to define the phrase culture of poverty is to ascribe to it a set of habits, modes of thinking, values held, and ways of acting that develop over a period of time because of historic, societal, and economic factors that have kept a given group in an isolated development, which in turn, magnifies those habits between group members when it remains in

	POVERTY	MIDDLE CLASS	WEALTH
POSSESSIONS	People	Things	One-of-a-kind objects, legacies, pedigrees
MONEY	To be used, spent	To be managed	To be conserved, invested
PERSONALITY	Is for entertainment. Sense of humor is highly valued	Is for acquisition and stability. Achievement is highly valued	Is for connections. Financial, political, social connections are highly valued
SOCIAL EMPHASIS	Social inclusion of people he/she likes	Emphasis is on self-governance and self-sufficiency	Emphasis is on social exclusion
FOOD	Key question: Did you have enough? Quantity important	Key question: did you like it? Quality important	Key question: Was it presented well? Presentation important
CLOTHING	Clothing valued for individual style and expression of personality	Clothing valued for its quality and acceptance into norm of middle class. Label important	Clothing valued for its artistic sense and expression. Designer important
TIME	Present most important. Decisions made for moment based on feelings or survival	Future most important. Decisions made against future ramifications	Traditions and history most important. Decisions made partially on basis of tradition and decorum

EDUCATION	Valued and revered as abstract but not as reality	Crucial for climbing success ladder and making money	Necessary tradition for making and maintaining connections
DESTINY	Believes in fate. Cannot do much to mitigate chance	Believes in choice. Can change future with good choices now	Noblesse oblige
LANGUAGE	Casual register. Language is about survival	Formal register. Language is about negotiation	Formal register. Language is about networking
FAMILY STRUCTURE	Tends to be matriarchal	Tends to be patriarchal	Depends on who has money
WORLD VIEW	Sees world in terms of local setting	See world in terms of national setting	Sees world in terms of international view
LOVE	Love and acceptance conditional, based upon whether individual is liked	Love and acceptance conditional and based largely upon achievement	Love and acceptance conditional and related to social standing and connections
DRIVING FORCES	Survival, relationships, entertainment	Work, achievement	Financial, political, social connections
HUMOR	About people and sex	About situations	About social faux pas

force over multiple generations. Such a special culture has developed in the small segment of the African-American community we label the underclass in our inner-city communities. It did not develop overnight and many forces combined to give it substance.

Three hundred years of American slavery were followed by decades of Jim Crowism, which were followed by more decades of racism, discrimination, and subpar education. Then many of these black communities were left behind because of structural, economic, and technological changes that eliminated manufacturing jobs and left people jobless, uneducated, and increasingly poor. These conditions accelerated family breakdown, rising illegitimacy, violence, crime, and ways of thinking and acting that were observed by each new generation who, in turn, continued and perpetuated these same things as adults. Thus was born this culture of poverty.

This social and residential isolation offers no role models for middle-class values, attitudes, or behaviors. Surveys have shown that residents in such communities outwardly accept American values, such as hard work and the importance of education, but they do not live up to or act on them. Negative behaviors, such as early sex and out-of-wedlock births happen everywhere, but the difference in ghetto communities is that there are no forces of social organization strong enough to check these actions, and thus they are transmitted to the young over a number of generations. Psychologists report that the sense of inability to influence, control, or change things in such an environment leads to feelings of anxiety, hopelessness, and futility.

Harvard sociologist William Julius Wilson's studies of such communities has led him to conclude that this cultural transmission happens because the individual's exposure to attitudes and behaviors happens with such frequency that they consciously or subconsciously become a part of that individual's own perspective on life and society. The overall result is a way of life that is peculiar to these isolated ghetto communities and quantitatively and qualitatively different from that of the American middle class.

This specific culture manifests itself in numerous ways. The residential isolation and population density of many inner-city communities fosters problems. As early as 1834, Charles Loring Brace, the head of New York City's Children's Aid Society, claimed that the increasing population density of American cities had eroded the character of the inhabitants, saying, "The very condensing of their numbers within a small space seems to stimulate their bad tendencies."

In previous times young black people were more likely to derive their identity and value from their church and family. Too often today the media, entertainment, and sports are the major forces of cultural transmission to all youth but especially to inner-city black young people, who most often have no positive role models in their neighborhoods or in their lives. Hip-hop culture has openly promoted the most oppositional ways of life against middle-class norms, celebrating gangsta rap, widespread promiscuous sexuality, and lack of regard for responsible paternity. In our inner cities we have seen the development of a subculture in which many young men take pride in the number of their sexual exploits, are contemptuous of conventional family life, find a sense of manhood in impregnating but not marrying women, and settle their conflicts and disagreements through violent means.

As I write this book in late 2012, Chicago is the topic of national concern because of the dramatic increase in killings. Two hundred fifty-nine homicides occurred during the first six months of this year. A breakdown of those numbers reveals that more than 200 of those murders were of African-Americans, forty-four were Hispanic, eleven were white, and three were Asian. The overwhelming number of those killings took place in the south and west portions of the city, the areas of the most concentrated and isolated low socioeconomic African-American residents.

This behavior has found its way into the schools as well. Dozens of victims have been victims of shootings. Chicago teachers have been punched, kicked, and attacked by groups of students. In Cook County, where Chicago is located, there were 21,806 reported attacks on teachers in 2012, a 44 percent increase from the year 2000 and far above those reported in the counties surrounding Chicago. Today schools are required to adhere to specific legal guidelines and due process prior to suspending or expelling students. These are good and necessary safeguards for students against arbitrary actions by school officials, but they have also hampered the ability of school administrators to take the necessary steps to protect both faculty and students.

Educators have been criticized for administering suspensions and expulsions in disproportionate numbers to African-American students. Statistics reveal that the percentages of student expulsions by race are 35 percent blacks, 20 percent Hispanics, 15 percent whites, and 12 percent Asians. No doubt the percentage of black students has exceeded other students, and in some instances this may have happened because of racism and discrimination, but the facts are that African-American students are responsible for a disproportionate number of school infractions. Many of these disciplinary actions are the result of those cultural factors we have been exploring in this chapter. The National Institute of Justice survey of students in ten high schools in Illinois, California, New Jersey, and Louisiana found that 22 percent of students possessed guns, 12 percent carried those guns most of the time, and 23 percent carry their weapons some of the time. The President's Commission on the causes of crime and the prevention of violence reported that blacks had committed 72 percent of homicides, 74 percent of aggravated assaults, 81 percent of unarmed robberies, and 85 percent of armed robberies.

This review of crime and violence statistics merely underscores some of the many unfortunate results of living in a world of poverty and discrimination, which forces individuals to live in isolated enclaves where such behaviors are common and are models for the young as to what actions are tolerable and even acceptable. Over multiple generations these conditions have fostered what has been identified as an oppositional culture in which middle-class norms and values are not understood, valued, or followed. Instead, a different set of rules for living takes their place. Students, then, often bring this oppositional set of values into the classroom, which conflicts with the expectations of the middle-class values of the schools and often leads to student failure, dropouts, and high incidences of discipline problems. The culture of street smarts and the code of the street become the rule book that students in these underclass communities often choose to follow.

Because there are so few avenues in which young people can earn respect, gaining that respect is a high priority that is often achieved by having brand-name clothes, jackets, or shoes; or by showing one's manhood through violence or sexual conquests; or by speaking in a particular manner. In the minds of some African-American youth, this priority of gaining respect takes precedence over anything the school has to offer.

A highly respected panel of the National Academy of Science estimated that one-fourth of all American youth are at serious risk of not becoming successful adults because of out-of-wedlock births, failure to finish high school, criminal or delinquent behavior, or substance abuse. African-American young people in our inner cities tragically fit many parts of that warning because they have among the highest levels of school dropouts and have found themselves in situations in which one-third of them are born to women who have never reached the ninth grade.

It is important to stress again that what is being discussed here is not race but rather a specific subculture, not only of the general overall American middle class but also specifically of the African-American middle class. It is also important to repeat for emphasis that blacks from the West Indies are clearly examples, based upon their lifestyle and accomplishments, of individuals who have not been shaped by the inner-city culture of poverty. What is striking to anyone living or visiting New York City is that the cab drivers and street vendors are black but, overwhelmingly, not native-born blacks. Their concept of work and entrepreneurship is a stark contrast to the lack of such values among African-Americans of the same social class. Blacks from the West Indies have lower crime rates than African-Americans and actually lower crime rates than white Americans. By the second generation of living in the United States, they have achieved a standard of living and educational level that exceed the national average, and their children outperform African-American black children in school.

The story of the immigrant West Indies black population makes a strong argument that the dysfunction of inner-city black neighborhoods and schools is not a function of race or genetics but is rather the result of a culture that has developed and has been perpetuated over time. The academic achievement of Chinese-Americans also is evidence of the power of a culture that derived from a long history of valuing education, learning, and scholarship in China, where the most learned men were at the top of the social hierarchy.

The lack of achievement of African-American students cannot be exclusively blamed on the culture of poverty but also on a general cultural condition affecting all students of every socioeconomic class. Our nation has a long history of anti-intellectualism in which those who "did something" were historically valued more than those who "knew something." Presidential candidates, for example, seemingly cannot be overly intellectual. Adlai Stevenson was classified as an egghead, and President Barack Obama is accused of being too professorial.

Today the typical American high school student spends approximately four hours per week doing schoolwork at home, while in other industrialized countries students average four hours per day doing such academic work at home. Surveys report that one of six students deliberately tries to hide his or her intelligence for fear of being ridiculed or rejected by other students. More than half of American students say they never discuss any aspect of their school-work with friends, and when asked what group they would like to be part of, five times as many students say the "populars" as opposed to those known as the "brains."

Studies of how American teenagers spend their time indicate that about 15 percent of their time, including class time, is spent on learning. Similar longitudinal studies have revealed that the longer a particular immigrant student's family has lived in the United States, the worse those students perform in school. Thus, it is common that foreign-born students earn higher grades than American-born students. The impact of the American anti-intellectual environment affects virtually every ethnic group. In the United States, native-born Cubans, Japanese, Mexican, Asians, and African-Americans are surpassed academically by immigrant students from those countries. A great deal of academic research, with mixed results, has been devoted to the theory that one of the reasons for the poor academic achievement of American black students is that if they do well in school, they will be chastised by their fellow African-American peers for acting white, implying that academic achievement is something negative that they associate with white middle-class values, which they reject.

Thus, the concept of culture, both that specific culture of poverty associated with the black underclass and the general anti-intellectual American culture, work together to discourage and impede higher levels of academic achievement. But if the culture of poverty has evolved over generations because of isolation and poverty itself, might it be possible to alter that culture by giving individuals financial and institutional assistance that will elevate their economic status equal to that of the middle class? Susan E. Mayer, a professor of public policy at Harvard University, explored this issue in her book *What Money Can't Buy: Family Income and Children's Life Chances.* What Mayer found reinforces the fact that a culture of poverty is, in fact, a reality and that merely increasing income in the inner-city underclass neighborhoods will have a minimal effect on values and behavior that will lead to success in school or in life. Here are some of her important findings regarding what simply giving more income to persons at the poverty level will do:

- Children's test scores are likely to improve by only one or two points

- There would likely be a one-tenth decline in out-of-wedlock births
- Doubling the parent's income might increase the years a child would remain in school by around one-fifth of a year
- Doubling low income families' income would reduce high school dropout rates by 1 percent

One might argue that those results would be welcomed developments, but we would have to admit, as well, that these figures represent an exceptionally small dividend for the money that would be required to be expended. What Mayer is saying is that even doubling income levels would not result in the instant transformation of those chronically poor people into the ranks of the American middle class in terms of attitudes, values, and beliefs. Mayer says, "When almost all employers discriminated against blacks, it was not surprising that blacks were more likely than whites to be poor. The fact that most blacks now escape long-term poverty leads one to the suspicion that those blacks who remain poor today are different from those who do better…. Unlike the short-term poor, the long-term poor tend to be quite different from the non-poor." Mayer concludes her study by saying that if we want to improve children's outcomes in school and in life the need is to study not only the effect of income but, as importantly, the effect of "non-economic characteristics." This, she admits, is no easy task. "Values and attitudes are like habits," she says. "The longer one adheres to them the harder they are to change." She concludes her book with this important sentence: "The results of this book suggest that although children's opportunities are unequal, income inequality is not the primary reason." Although she doesn't use the phrase, what she means is that the primary reason is culture and particularly a culture born of long-term isolated poverty.

So in our exploration of the underlying causes of the black-white achievement gap, culture stands out as a key, if not the most important, element. It is a culture developed from many sources we have discussed in previous chapters. It was formed by the African heritage, American slavery, and Jim Crowism, continued racism, and segregation and made almost permanent in inner-city communities by a change in the economy that decimated manufacturing jobs and by technology that has left all but the educated even further behind. The culture of poverty continues to impact the academic achievement of too many African-American inner-city students.

Thus, if we have correctly identified the essence of the problem, we can now attempt to seek solutions to the achievement gap of the largest group of underachieving African-American students. But we should proceed with some caution. As we reported earlier, the black-white achievement gap is not only a condition of underclass ghetto communities. We need to recall that black students underperform in relation to white students in every state in which the National Assessment of Educational Progress is given; they also underperform whites at every socioeconomic level from the poor to the middle class to the wealthy. The concept of culture is an important step in understanding underachievement for a particular sector of the black community, but it does not fully explain the full scope of the achievement gap. This incomplete explanation, as well as the general problem of bringing about educational change of any kind, signals that the road to closing the achievement gap will be neither quick nor easy.

CHAPTER IX

TROUBLING PROSPECTS FOR A COMPLEX PROBLEM

I deally one would hope to complete this exploration into the various elements of the achievement gap with a happy, or at least hopeful, conclusion. Unfortunately, for the issue of the black-white achievement gap, there are no quick, easy, and totally satisfactory solutions. This does not mean that some things cannot be done, since to do nothing is a sure formula for a negative future for millions of young people as well as for our nation. In the following chapters we will explore some steps that must be taken to close the achievement gap, but first, in this chapter, it is important to review those solutions we have already attempted, too often with limited success, and also to address those forces that are major obstacles to change.

A recent report by the education reform group A+, which discussed the achievement gap in just one state, Pennsylvania, concluded that the gap was very slowly decreasing, but at the rate of current movement it will take forty years to close that gap. Forty years! It is doubtful that our nation can maintain its current position as a global economic and military leader with four more decades of high school dropouts and graduates incapable of reading a newspaper or doing simple math or having the basic skills to qualify for a job. Outside our borders there is also a cloud of pessimism regarding the immediate capacity to close the achievement gap. In England, a report entitled "Failure by Any Other Name" stated that "no single government policy has successfully closed the gap in educational attainment and black pupils continue to be associated with educational disadvantage and failure." Reports from France, Germany, and the Netherlands show their efforts to reduce educational inequalities have had only modest success. In Brazil the underachievement of black students has also not been resolved. What about our own country?

Our earlier review of the experience of immigrant groups with schools revealed that, in fact, the schools seldom worked for most of them. Non-school attendance and elementary and high school dropout rates were extremely high. When students were different from the prevailing norm, whether as a result of race, nationality, or culture, their academic success rates for the first or second generations were not high. It was only when two key things happened that the children and grandchildren of southern and eastern European immigrants began to be successful in school. The first was when the parents of those students became economically stable and could count themselves as moving toward or being part of the middle class. That is, economic success was a necessary first step toward academic success. Second, the children and grandchildren of these immigrants succeeded as they lost their "differentness" and in appearance, language, and behavior took on the norms and values of white middle-class America. Obviously for African-Americans today, the one ingredient in that formula they cannot emulate deals with the issue of race, although it is considerably less a barrier today than it was even a generation ago.

Over the past fifty years our nation has committed untold millions and millions of dollars to targeted educational and community programs to address the achievement gap issue. Yet with all such expenditures we have not as yet solved the problem. The federal Title I program had spent over thirteen billion dollars by 2007 on programs to assist poor, mostly minority children, yet no evaluation of Title I since the 1970s onward has found any strong evidence that the expenditure of money on these programs has had a significant positive impact on student achievement. In fact, a 2001 study by the U.S. Department of Education revealed that the gap had widened from 1986 to 1999. The federal Head Start Program has shown success in areas such as physical health programs, but student initial academic gains begin to fade away in late elementary school. Even programs such as Early Head Start, which begin at birth and continue to age three, have not proven to be successful at improving later academic outcomes. Other early childhood programs such as the Perry Program and the Milwaukee Project have shown some positive results, but they can be costly at about $14,000 per student in 2007 dollars. Estimates of the cost of expanding such early intervention programs have been over $103 billion dollars. Given current economic conditions, the prospects for such a massive infusion of dollars appears to be slim.

The No Child Left Behind (NCLB) federal legislation, which had the lofty, idealistic, and unachievable goal of closing the achievement gap by 2014, is but another example of good intentions gone bad. It has not come close to achieving its goal and has had numerous unintended negative results. It has been, first of all, an unprecedented involvement—some would say intrusion—of the federal government in the sphere of education for which the government has no constitutional authority. One can legitimately argue that the twenty-first century world requires some kind of unified, consistent, national, high quality educational system, and only the federal government can bring this about. The fact remains, however, that the U.S. Constitution gives the federal government absolutely no role in education. Historically, education has been a state responsibility. Thus, before even the merits or demerits of any legislation to close the achievement gap are debated, the proper role of the federal government regarding schools is a potential obstacle that must be defined or further clarified. The current No Child Left Behind legislation has created high-stakes testing anxiety in every school district and in every teacher across the country. Schools have been closed down and teachers left unemployed because of low scores on state assessments. The percentage of teachers leaving the profession within the first five years of their employment has increased, and teachers, in certain communities, have been subjected to public ridicule when their names are published in local newspapers as being among the worst in regard to their student's test scores. This public reporting of test scores is made with no background information regarding the school's socioeconomic status or any special situations faced by students in those schools. Pressure to score well on reading and math on these tests has resulted in the shortchanging or elimination of subjects such as history, art, music, and even science as schools are forced to allocate time and money to subjects to be tested and publicly reported. Scandals, such as widespread cheating on tests in Atlanta and elsewhere, underscore the enormous pressure educators face regarding the No Child Left Behind legislation when, in fact, it has been a failure in closing the achievement gap. The NCLB legislation also allowed each state to develop its own tests. The result has been scores that mean little because comparisons are impossible between states: some have developed tests that are easier than those in other states.

This obsession with test scores has totally ignored any measurement of non-cognitive skills. Things such as character traits and citizenship are not measured even though surveys of Americans report that the school's role in teaching values is more important than their role in teaching academic subjects. The black-white gap in terms of student behavior is also a concern of educators, since black students exhibit more anti-social behavior from preschool to the high school years.

Studies have shown that academic test scores can explain only about one-fifth of the relationship between increased schooling and higher earnings. The remaining four-fifths of those variables are never tested on current academic assessments. Fortunately, the Obama administration responded to some of these problems, and states can now apply for certain waivers from the current law, which is still, at this writing, in need of a complete overhaul. If there is one important lesson here, it is that everything we know about the history and origins of the black-white achievement gap should tell us that it cannot be legislated away.

The high stakes testing environment in which we currently live not only has failed to close the achievement gap but also has ignored other things we now know about learning and future success. Research dealing with the fact that not all of us learn in the same manner—that some of us learn through reading, others by audio or visual presentations, and others by different means—is not addressed in how we measure the achievement gap or in our teaching strategies. Unless this theory of multiple intelligences is addressed, it is unlikely that we will ever get a handle on the true scope of the achievement gap. The private sector is far ahead of our schools in recognizing the importance of yet another type of intelligence never measured in state tests, that being the concept of emotional intelligence (EI). Emotional intelligence is a recognition that IQ and standardized tests fail to evaluate aspects that, in the long run, are likely to be more important to a student's success. As was cited earlier, some of the key aspects of EI are self-awareness, the ability to be aware of and in touch with one's own feelings and emotions, self-regulation, capacity to manage various emotions, self-motivation, and empathy as well as having the interpersonal skills to build positive relationships with others.

For some who seek to close the achievement gap, the answer lies in doing something to make schools culturally responsive. Some critics argue, for example, that achievement tests are culturally biased, and this results in African-American students having poor test scores. This argument reached an extreme phase when, in 1979, a California court banned the use of IQ tests in public schools—but the ban applied only to black students. White, Asian, Hispanic, and Native American students were unaffected by the ban, with obviously no consideration of the fact that if the tests were culturally biased, it could impact these other groups as well. Almost twenty years later, in Oakland, California, a claim was made that most of the black students were not native speakers of English, that, in fact, they spoke some version of black English labeled Ebonics. In recognition of this contention and to implement its inclusion in the schools, the Los Angeles Unified School District allocated three million dollars, which was wasted money because the program resulted in no positive results in black academic achievement.

Other culturally responsive moves have also had little success. Some schools with predominantly African-American students adopted an Afro-centric curriculum that they believed would interest students more and enable them to have a positive identification with what they were learning. The positive identification of students with various aspects of their past and present cultures and history is a very positive thing, but there is really no evidence that these Afro-centric-themed schools have dramatically raised achievement scores and closed the achievement gap. No other racial or ethnic group has asked for schools with a unique curriculum based on the group's race or ethnicity, yet these other groups have adapted reasonably well to the standard American school structure and curriculum. Unfortunately, the same has been true regarding black control of their schools. Arguments that African-Americans needed to control their own schools so that they could initiate programs and strategies to help students achieve have not proven to be the valid. Places such as Detroit; Gary, Indiana; East St. Louis, Illinois; and dozens of other medium and small black-controlled school districts have not fared well academically.

The need for more qualified African-American teachers with whom black students can identify does have merit, although the evidence is scant that black students who have black teachers do substantially better than those who have white teachers. The fact that black teachers can be role models for students is important and cannot be dismissed, particularly in those inner-city communities where there are so few positive roles models of any kind. This issue has once again become complicated by a paradox of progress. The crumbling of the historic high walls of prejudice and discrimination in our nation has created opportunities for educated African-Americans that were previously closed to them. Today young college-educated black men and women are studying for MBA degrees, going to law and medical schools, and receiving PhDs. Teaching in elementary and high school is seldom on the priority list of top students as they plan their careers and futures. The current condition of teaching as a profession further discourages talented young black men and women. As was noted earlier, surveys of college students report that academically top students are not planning to teach because of concerns that they would have trouble financially if they chose the profession as well as the fact that they did not view teaching as a profession that rewards excellence. These conditions make it clear that the prospects of getting the most talented students of any race to choose teaching as a career are not promising.

Other school-based strategies have been tried as well but with disappointing results. Grouping students by ability has both proponents and detractors. Some feel it allows for students to be given the specialized instruction needed to address academic deficits, while others view the practice as one that perpetuates labeling and discrimination. No one has presented evidence that the practice has closed the achievement gap. Reducing class size does have a positive impact in the first elementary grades, but those gains seem to disappear as students progress to the upper grades. Desegregation of public schools, while a necessary and just action that had to be done, has also not closed the academic achievement gap. Black students attending previously all white or mixed race schools, some in the most affluent school districts, still fall behind whites on the state academic assessments.

The national movement to provide school choice through charter schools and vouchers has also had limited success. Vouchers continue to be the exception rather than the rule in education and thus far have produced no substantial evidence that the voucher schools do anything more to close the achievement gap than is done by traditional public schools. Opposition to voucher programs remains strong in most of the nation, so it is unlikely that we will see any major expansion of the voucher idea in the immediate future. The charter school movement is now more than twenty years old; but if charter schools were the vehicle to close the achievement gap, they have yet to fulfill that promise. The overall record of charter schools in the nation is very mixed. Many are doing well with encouraging results in closing the gap, but here, too, they are the exception and not the rule.

The hope that successful charter schools would be a stimulant to bring new ideas into the public schools has yet to materialize. Even the hope of what charter schools might do when freed from some bureaucratic restraints is being dashed by the concerted efforts of the public school establishment to reduce any bureaucratic freedoms and impose additional requirements and restrictions on charter schools, which are making them look increasingly very much like the standard, traditional public schools. The fundamental idea behind charter schools was an implicit agreement—charter schools would be given freedom from numerous school rules and regulations so that they could be free to innovate and try new educational approaches. In return for that freedom they would be subject to a higher level of accountability—if they did not show academic growth and achievement or if they were financially mismanaged, they would be shut down.

This was an exciting opportunity and one with a chance to do things the regular public schools could not do because of their regulatory restrictions. It was also a more risky venture because these schools could actually be closed, and everyone working at the school would lose their employment, a scenario seldom seen in regular public schools where miserable performance can go on for decades with no penalties imposed. But today that previous opportunity to do something different or innovative is quickly disappearing. City school districts require virtually the same rules and bureaucratic reports as they require for all their schools. Charter authorizers require an unprecedented number of reports and documents to approve a charter. State departments of education announce rules and regulations to which all schools must adhere. And the federal government, first with the No Child Left Behind requirements and now with Common Core Standards, has also aggressively moved to reduce the idea of options and choice by establishing requirements and a curriculum that will be standardized throughout the country. So it is doubtful that individuals seeking to address the black-white achievement gap through innovation in charter schools will have much leeway in the future. And, of course, teachers unions have never been supportive of the creation or expansion of charter schools and have not, unfortunately, directly addressed the academic gap issue by offering any specific proposals or strategies.

A few high-profile reports have been published with stories of specific schools that have purportedly had success in closing the achievement gap. The conservative-leaning Heritage Foundation published a small book identifying twenty-one high-poverty schools that had achievement levels above the national norm. But Richard Rothstein, the former education writer for the *New York Times*, challenged the stories, citing the fact that only six of the twenty-one schools were non-selective enrollment schools, and even those six were a miniscule example when the U.S. Department of education identified more than 7,000 high-poverty and low-performing schools in the country. Rothstein also pointed out that these so-called successful schools only highlighted academic scores in the primary grades and did not report declining scores in the upper grades. The more liberal-leaning Education Trust cited 1,320 schools that had at least 50 percent black students and scored in the top one-third in their state. Rothstein also challenged this report of supposed success. His analysis revealed that the schools cited had high academic scores in only one grade, in only one subject, and for only one year—hardly a major educational achievement.

Certain charter schools have, with extensive publicity, also claimed great success in educating African-American students. These schools boast of sending 90 percent to 100 percent of their graduates on to college. That fact, in itself, is certainly to be praised and applauded. What is not reported is that a high percentage of the students who started at those schools as freshmen never made it to their senior year and never graduated. The reported ACT scores of the graduating students are also low and raise serious doubts regarding the potential success of these students in a four-year university program without extensive remedial assistance. The Kipp charter schools have also received national press coverage that has been positive regarding their education of minorities. Their school model is unique, and it is commendable that they have achieved whatever success they have, but it is not a model that has any hope of being duplicated on a large national scale or being adopted by the various large urban public school systems. A school day that runs between eight and nine hours with additional Saturday classes and with twenty-four-hour, on-call teachers will not find widespread public support.

Various scholars who have studied the achievement gap have also come to disheartening conclusions. The famous Coleman Report, it will be recalled, found that the quality of schools explained little about differences in academic achievement. Coleman found that factors such as the credentials of the teachers, curriculum, physical facilities, and the amount of money expended per student were not as important as family backgrounds of the students. Lawrence Steinberg concluded that the school was only one influence, and probably not the most important one, that affects what students learn and how they perform on achievement tests. His recommendation is that we should begin to examine these academic disparities by looking at students' lives outside of school. Jencks and Phillips, in their detailed study of the black-white achievement gap concluded that "cognitive disparities between white and black schoolchildren are currently so large that it is hard to imagine how schools alone could eliminate them." Richard Rothstein, in his book *Class and Schools,* wrote that "no matter how competent the teacher, the academic achievement of lower class children will, on average, almost inevitably be less than that of middle class children."

In 1999 the school superintendents of fourteen urban school districts in the United States came together and formed the Minority Student Achievement Network (MSAN) so that there could be an exchange of ideas and support in the effort to find answers and solutions to closing the black-white achievement gap. These districts were located in different states, and their average per-pupil expenditures exceeded the state per-pupil expenditure averages. These communities, such as Berkley, California; Cambridge, Massachusetts; Chapel Hill, North Carolina; Ann Arbor, Michigan; and Evanston and Oak Park, Illinois, had tried various approaches and strategies with little success. It was hoped that this collaborative approach would have better luck in discovering some answers as to how to close the achievement gap. Although such an approach makes sense, as yet there is no evidence that these communities and school leaders have discovered the answers they have sought.

Obstacles to resolving the black-white gap are clearly huge, and any who claim quick or easy answers should be approached with skepticism and extreme caution. But if doing nothing or continuing to follow the same failed strategies is not an option, what can we do? Those who quickly dismiss the school itself as impotent to act are unnecessarily writing off the importance of the school. On the other hand, those who believe the schools alone can close that gap have ignored our history or suffer from an unsupported and incurable optimism. Things can and must be done, but they are not easy, and they will not be comfortable for some.

CHAPTER X

WHAT IS TO BE DONE? THE ROLE OF PUBLIC POLICY

So where are we? Considering all the potential causes of the achievement gap we have explored, and the obstacles for change we have identified, what lessons can we learn, and what solutions for closing that gap are possible?

We have seen that history is important and that our educational history tells us that schools in America have never done too well with those who were not initially middle-class, white, Anglo-Saxon Protestants. The previous sentence is not a racist or un-American statement; it is simply a verified fact. That is why Irish immigrants were looked down upon, German immigrants lobbied for German to be the language of some of their schools, and Catholic immigrants established a large alternative parochial school system in our nation. So again, we must remind those who ask why so many black students can't make it in our schools when so many poor European immigrant students did that, in fact, most of those immigrant students did not do well in our schools. We have also seen that poverty and racism are important elements that play into the lack of academic achievement of black students. Those things alone, however, cannot be full explanations because European and Asian immigrants lived in dire poverty and faced violence and extreme discrimination from the native white American majority and still successfully overcame those obstacles. We have also seen that contemporary Asian children living in or near poverty conditions continue to do very well academically, while black children coming from affluent homes and communities still do not meet the academic achievement levels of white or Asian students from that same socioeconomic group. Our review of the evidence has also established that while the amount of money supporting education was an element of great disparity between black and white schools in the past, it is no longer the case. In fact, many predominantly black urban school systems receive substantially more money than other districts yet still report some of the lowest academic results.

Our history has also reminded us that in the past we were quick to label southern and eastern European immigrants as retarded, because they did so poorly on IQ tests. Yet their descendants are today among the most educated and successful Americans. The claim that those groups were not genetically equipped to succeed in school was wrong then and, as evidence has shown, is wrong now. There is no scientifically credible and accepted evidence that African-Americans are genetically intellectually inferior to whites or Asians or anyone else, and the overwhelming number of examples of black academic, social, and financial success should dispel such explanations.

The complex connection between the inner-city poor black underclass family and the culture developed over time in those communities is something that has had a profound impact on the lack of academic success of so many black students. We have seen that every socioeconomic group in America— the poor, the middle class, and the very rich—do, in fact, create their own subculture within the overall American culture. To acknowledge that there are cultural elements that are particular to the urban black underclass that contribute to a lack of school success is not a statement to blame the victim but, rather, a statement of fact recognized by anyone who has the experience of living, working, or teaching in those poor minority communities. This cultural element is a key to understanding black student underachievement and to finding solutions to it.

If then we are to seek answers for closing the achievement gap, we need to address the issues surrounding culture head-on while at the same time keeping our eye on our past history for lessons that can guide us. The road to closing the achievement gap must be a dual one that eventually merges into one clear path. We need first to look at some things that must be done in the larger arena of American society that could allow schools to do their job more effectively. Then we must look at the schools themselves and identify what drastic changes are needed if this achievement gap is ever to be closed. Those dual paths will be difficult to travel, and we will not have an overnight solution to the achievement gap problem.

Perhaps the first thing that must be done is for our leaders once again to reaffirm the basic, powerful idea that is the essence of or nation, that is, the one we summarize as the American Dream. That idea affirms that we are committed as a nation to the principle of equal opportunity. What has made us unique and exceptional as a nation is the idea that if people are given equal opportunity, there are no limits to where an individual's energy, commitment, brains, and pure hard work can take them. This is quite different from promising equality of results. Such a promise or doctrine not only is not part of our past history, it is also unattainable in the real world. We must close the academic achievement gap between blacks and whites because that gap is so large, and the consequences of not closing it are so serious. That does not mean that every single black, white, Hispanic, Asian, and Native American child will attain equal scores on state tests or on any other assessment. Closing that gap means that, given the right conditions and policies of both society and schools, we will reach a condition in which black children are not consistently behind white children; at the same time it will not be uncommon for some white children to outperform blacks, but it will also not be uncommon for some black children to out-perform whites. So what are some things that we as a society must do to create the condition of equal opportunity?

Nothing we can do will be more important than to create economic conditions in our nation that will allow adult black men to become employed. As long as there are large numbers of unemployed black men spending their days and nights on the streets of our inner-city neighborhoods, the academic gap will never be closed. This needs to be repeated. Unless these men have jobs, the gap will never be closed. These men need jobs for their own economic well-being, for their sense of self-esteem, and, per-haps most important, for women to see them as re-sponsible partners suitable for marriage and family life. But matching these men with jobs will not be easy. The large percentage of unemployed black men with limited education are living in an economic en-vironment in which only those with specialized skills or college degrees can fill available jobs, and most of these men have neither of those credentials. There are relatively few responses to such a situation, but something must be done.

First, the leaders of the black community—church pastors, the NAACP, the Urban League, the black political leadership—must convince the unemployed that there is honor in work itself, any kind of work. If uneducated Hispanic men can do lawn maintenance, so, too, can black men. If adult Hispanic men can be busboys and short-order cooks in our restaurants, so, too, can black men. If uneducated immigrant Polish women who can hardly speak English can do housecleaning, so, too, can black men and women.

Second, our federal, state, and city governments must create programs to stimulate and encourage black entrepreneurship. If uneducated Arab immigrants can open small grocery stores, and uneducated Asian Indians can open donut shops, and uneducated Korean immigrants can open dry cleaning establishments, so, too, can black uneducated men and women.

Third, our government agencies must continue to require work for public assistance as well as to provide public sector jobs to employ these large numbers of unemployed men. Our roads are in disrepair, our bridges are in dangerous conditions, our city streets are filled with junk and debris and need cleaning, our schools need new paint and repairs, and the list of needs goes on and on. As a nation we must develop a manufacturing strategy for the twentieth-first century. A rebirth of manufacturing will be a legitimate avenue for employment of these undereducated men who now fill our inner-city streets. Given the exceptionally large number of school dropouts, these seem to be the only avenues available to us, and doing these things will have a direct impact on closing the achievement gap as the potential for stable two-parent black families grows.

In both the short and long runs, the most important thing that must be done to close the achievement gap of black students is to create conditions that contribute to the formation of economically stable middle-class black families. If men in our inner-city communities are gainfully employed, they will become desirable prospects for women who desire security and family life. Obviously, in today's economic conditions, these scores of unemployed men are hardly desirable prospects for marriage, and the result has been dramatically increased numbers of out-of-wedlock births and single mothers, who, too often, find themselves trapped in poverty. Unless some semblance of two-parent family structure is brought back to the African-American inner-city community, the other policies, most of which have been tried and failed, will have minimal impact on raising the achievement levels of black inner-city children. The reason for this is that such family structures take on the discipline and values of the American middle class and provide an antidote to all the negative conditions children who live in inner–city, violence-prone poverty conditions face. It is stable, middle-class environments that characterize the lives of successful African-Americans who are now part of that American middle and upper middle class. And once again we need to remember the lessons of our history. The only time poverty-stricken, non-English-speaking ethnic immigrants began to be successful in our schools was when they had first achieved some economic and family stability and gradually accepted and practiced American middle-class values and lifestyles.

Harvard scholar Isabel Sawhill's research has identified four steps that must be taken to virtually eliminate the chance that a child will be born into poverty and remain in poverty. The four steps are easy to list but, given the cultural problems that have developed in our African-American inner-city communities, much harder to achieve. These simple steps for individuals are: (1) graduate from high school, (2) have no children until marriage, (3) get married, (4) obtain steady employment. By following these steps, those individuals will then have only a 1 percent chance of ever finding themselves in an economic condition of poverty. Taking these four steps would be a major step in the right direction, but something more would be required as well to impact the success of black children in our schools. As we recounted earlier, Susan E. Mayer, in her insightful book *What Money Can't Buy: Family Income and Children's Life Chances,* demonstrated that the addition of more income, whether by welfare assistance or by employment, is not enough to create the values that parents must have and must convey to their children if those children are to succeed in school and in life. Mayer said that those remaining in a culture of poverty for two, three, four, or more generations have developed a different set of values that are, in many ways, the opposite of middle-class norms and values of the larger society and of the schools. Mayer puts it this way, "Unlike the short term poor, the long term poor tend to be quite different from the non-poor... Thus if the state equalizes the most important material and pedagogical investments in children, social and psychological differences between parents will explain a larger percentage of the variation in the success of their children." In summary, what Mayer is saying is reflected in the title of her book. Money alone will have little impact on the life chances of inner-city poor black children, or anyone else for that matter, if they do not adopt and accept the values and lifestyles of the American middle class. This is unlikely to happen overnight simply because more African-American men have jobs, marry and have a family. Once again, there are no quick solutions to closing the achievement gap, but the reformation of families is an indispensable first step.

For some, this emphasis on accepting and acting on middle-class values goes against current calls for diversity and multiculturalism. There is value in both of those concepts, and schools must value and incorporate them, but they need not undermine the basic middle-class values that have characterized American public education from its real beginnings as an educational system in the mid-nineteenth century. Horace Mann's crusade to establish the American Common School had at its core the creation of an institution open to all who would be educated to accept and live their lives by certain values common to all Americans. Many immigrants from many lands were undoubtedly more comfortable with their own language, culture, ideas, and values. But they eventually determined that if they wanted to be accepted and have their children succeed in America, they did not have to abandon their roots and heritage,but they did, however, have to accept the values of the American middle class. When they did this, they, and particularly their children, began to succeed in our schools and in our nation. So a necessary first step in the long journey toward closing the black-white academic achievement gap is the restoration of the inner-city black family and the education of their children in the values that will be the foundation of their success, those being getting a good education, working hard, and following society's rules—meet those requirements, and the doors of opportunity will open. African-American author E. Franklin Frazier, writing in the 1930s about the Negro family, had it right when he concluded that the only way for blacks to form healthy families was to emulate American middle-class norms.

We also need to act on the research of James Coleman, which he presented to the country more than forty-seven years ago and which has not been seriously challenged or repudiated by other critical research for more than four decades. Coleman concluded that "the social composition of the student body is more highly related to achievement, independent of the child's own social background, than any other school factor." He found that school spending was not closely related to achievement but that the family's economic status was more predictive of that achievement and that going to school with middle-class peers offered a clear advantage for students, as opposed to attending a school with lower-class students. Coleman found that there was a tipping point at which all the negative influences of what we would identify as the culture of poverty became dominant. That tipping point occurred when a school had fewer than 60 percent of students who were from middle-class backgrounds and more than 40 percent who were from low-income families and that issues such as school discipline were strongly related to the percentage of lower-class students in a given classroom. Coleman concluded that racially integrating the schools was not nearly as important as integrating schools by socioeconomic ratios.

Today in the United States, eighty school districts are implementing plans to integrate their schools not by race but by socioeconomic status, with variation in percentages from what Coleman had suggested. In Wake County, North Carolina, for example, a policy has been created that calls for no more than 40 percent of students in a school being eligible for free and reduced lunch and no more than 25 percent of students reading below grade level. In another community, La Crosse, Wisconsin, a policy has been considered in which each school would have a free lunch population range of between 15 percent and 45 percent. No doubt such policies would still be opposed by some, and in urban centers such as Chicago or Detroit, where the numbers of students who are minority as well as being in a poverty status are exceptionally large, such models of socioeconomic integration would prove to be difficult. Nevertheless, it is a step worth trying where it is possible. Given the current environment in which the element of choice in our schools is more firmly established, it is probably more possible to structure this non-racial integration model than was the case when James Coleman issued his report. A recent book published by the Century Foundation, *The Future of School*

Integration: Socioeconomic Diversity as an Education Reform Strategy, maps out the poverty districts across the country and describes the possibilities for inter-district collaboration that would reduce the negative efforts that result from the isolation of students in high-poverty schools.

A number of steps will be required at the state and federal levels as well. The current effort in some states to raise the compulsory school attendance age to eighteen makes little sense. Unless we address the underlying reasons as to why students drop out of school when they legally can, raising the mandatory school attendance age will simply create a situation in which more young people are forced to attend an institution they find boring and irrelevant as it is currently structured, and the failure rate on state tests will soar even higher as will issues pertaining to school discipline and disruption. The only thing that would be accomplished would be to keep large numbers of persons out of the labor market a bit longer, but the lack of preparation for work or college will not have been fixed.

There are some positive proactive things our state and federal legislatures could do. Teacher education in our universities needs to address more specifically the special issues confronting inner-city, high-poverty, African-American schools. Few teachers complete their college preparation programs with any real depth of understanding of how to teach students to read, yet they will find the inability of their students to read will be their first and most pressing problem if they teach in a low-achieving minority school. Virtually no graduates of these teacher preparation programs have any knowledge, understanding, or experience in dealing with African-American inner-city communities, families, lifestyles, or values, and thus cultural conflicts between teachers and students are common.

We need to create financial incentives that encourage our very best teachers to take positions in these low-achieving schools. Programs should be legislated that ensure students in the academic top 10 percent of their high school graduating class are given full four-year scholarships to any state university in their state if they commit to teach for a minimum of five years in a low-achieving minority school. A stipulation must be made that if the individuals do not meet that commitment for any reason, they must repay the state the tuition subsidy they were given.

State legislatures and state departments of education need to create options for schools to try new and different approaches and not force everyone into uniform bureaucratic molds. Things such as Carnegie units, a concept now more than one hundred years old need to be reexamined, revised, or discarded. The important and powerful concept of choice needs to go beyond parents and students and be given to school administrators and school boards as well. States and school districts need to consider seriously the immediate and long-range consequences of continuing the high stakes testing environment currently operating in our nation. Places with high-achieving schools, such as Finland, seem to do exceptionally well without such tests. The fact that our schools have become test factories has clearly not closed the achievement gap but has instead narrowed the curriculum, made teachers frustrated and anxious, encouraged dishonesty, and most likely encouraged higher dropout rates as students see they cannot pass these tests. We certainly need to know what our schools are doing and whether our students are learning, but when we have reached the current situation in which 50 percent to 70 percent of the school day is spent on some form of test preparation and test taking, something is clearly wrong. States and districts must stop the practice of publicly grading and ranking schools, a practice that only serves to embarrass and stigmatize schools, districts, and teachers but does nothing to improve student academic growth. Thus far the strategy behind the high stakes testing movement has been one of coercion, threat, and punishment rather than one of support, reward, and recognition. What is clear is that policy makers who believe the achievement gap will be closed by punishments given when test scores are low have yet to show any evidence that such an approach has proven successful. What they should be doing is asking what is prohibiting academic success and then creating policies to eliminate obstacles and support needed change. Our policy makers need to ask what this excess of student testing tells us about the really important things that schools should be doing, such as fostering creativity; encouraging problem solving and critical thinking; teaching the value of resilience and persistence, reliability, and hard work; motivating; and promoting numerous other traits that will serve students well throughout their lives. If they would ask those questions, the answer would become readily clear that our current tests do nothing to assess any of those important issues.

The home and neighborhood environments of some of our African-American inner-city areas are so bad that in some select cases an even more drastic step must be taken if the talents and futures of young people are to be saved. Some students must be provided with the voluntary option of leaving those communities to live and learn in state-operated and state-funded boarding schools. To repeat, this cannot be a mandatory policy but rather another choice or option presented to a parent. Too often even the best practices of good schools have little impact when students return on a nightly basis to environments that are dangerous and gang-infested and to homes where there is little support or encouragement for anything related to school or academics. For many, such live-and-learn boarding facilities will be their only hope for survival. Facilities based on the famous Boy's Town model, started ninety years ago by Father Edward Flanagan, would be a good start. The Boy's Town model uses a five-step process of assessment, a customized training plan, consultation and technical support, evaluation, and sustainability to develop an effective educational program. The real value, though, to many hard to reach and teach young African-American students would be not only an environment where they could achieve academically but also a place where they would feel safe and would know that there was a way out of the dysfunctional environment in which so many are forced to live.

Finally, another public policy issue that needs reviewing is that of affirmative action. We need to set a specific date certain at which time the policy will end. Its original intent was justified, but it has it evolved into something it was never intended to be, namely, a quota system that fostered attitudes that have been more destructive than helpful. Whites began to resent it as a form of reverse discrimination that impacted them when persons with lesser credentials and abilities received a job, position, or college entrance before they did. And for some African-Americans, it caused self-doubt as they realized that they had been given preference not because of their abilities but rather because of the color of their skin. Discrimination still exists to be sure, but most barriers are down, and African-American students in our schools must now realize that affirmative action policies will not be their ticket to success. Instead, their education and ability will be what will open doors of opportunity in every field.

Our state and federal governments and institutions of higher learning, and no doubt others as well, must take the steps identified to create opportunities for the achievement gap to be reduced. Individual schools and school districts must take concrete steps as well.

CHAPTER XI

WHAT IS TO BE DONE? THE ROLE OF THE SCHOOLS

While the roles of government and society can have a major impact on closing the black-white achievement gap, schools themselves must take some important action steps as well. The role of schools should not be minimized. Schools do make a difference. The fact that students from similar socioeconomic and home backgrounds achieve at significantly different levels when they attend different schools is ample testimony to the importance of what schools actually do. In 1996 almost 75 percent of black students in fourth grade could not achieve at a basic level in mathematics, yet by 2007 the percentage of fourth graders at that underachieving level had fallen to 3 percent, a major, positive sign of academic growth. However, the achievement gap between white and black high school seniors is larger today than it was in the 1980s. As some have observed, all students, black and white, seem to learn less the longer they are in school. With less learning, the achievement gap gets larger. So what, if anything, can schools do?

As a start, schools need some concrete goals for all students—black, white, Hispanic, Asian, Native American, and anyone else. Some, but not all, of the issues surrounding the black-white achievement gap could be addressed by institutional changes that would benefit all students. At least six goals are appropriate for all schools. These goals are:

- All students will be grade proficient in basic skills and Common Core curriculum.
- All students will develop a sense of confidence and self-worth.
- All students will develop a sense of moral and ethical behavior.
- All students will develop a sense of reciprocal obligation to family, school, community, and country.
- All students will develop an appreciation and respect for various viewpoints, races, religions, and ethnic origins in our multicultural nation.
- All students will develop college/work/career competencies necessary to enable them to become productive members of the American global economy.

In order to achieve those goals, we need all of our schools to focus on a foundation of six pillars. These are relevance, rigor, engagement, choice, character, and competencies.

National surveys reveal that more than 40 percent of students said school was "boring" because the material wasn't relevant to their lives. A similar percentage said they "didn't see the value of the work they were asked to do." Relevance, then, must be a deliberate and conscious effort on the part of teachers to connect their teaching to the real world in which students live. The topic of relevance is worthy of numerous professional development sessions with teachers in every school, no matter what subjects they teach. These same surveys found that one-third of students said the material taught was "too easy," and two-thirds of high school students said they "would work harder if their schools offered more demanding and interesting courses."

Of students who said they have considered dropping out, more than 40 percent said they "didn't see the value of the work they were asked to do." Two-thirds of those students said they would have "worked harder" if more had been demanded of them. A first step in closing the achievement gap is to listen to students. They are not asking for ease or comfort or more fun in school. They are asking us to interest them, challenge them, respect them, and be creative in our teaching so that classes have relevance for their lives. Those are not unreasonable or unachievable requests. We cannot shy away from raising standards and truly believing that all students, black and white, can meet those standards when inspired, challenged, and supported by good teachers.

Our students are bored because of boring, stale, and outdated teaching practices. Lecturing to students and assessing their mindless rote memorization with multiple-choice tests are sure formulas for the dullest definition of what constitutes a good education. Students need to be actively engaged in problem solving, project creation, extensive writing, oral presentations, higher order thinking, and inquiry through team collaboration. Student engagement by creative teaching is a key to closing the achievement gap.

Students need choices as well. We all learn differently, yet, for the most part, we are all taught the same way. Our students will respond to options for acquiring and storing information and, as they mature through grades in school, what courses they are allowed to take. Giving students choices is empowering to them and gives them some control over their own learning.

Character education is also an important anchor of the curriculum. As we discussed in the last chapter, unless all students, particularly inner–city, underclass black students, understand, accept, and act out American middle-class values, their chances of success in college or in the marketplace are slim to none. Character education can fill this role by exposing students to analyzing concepts such as loyalty, honesty, promptness, commitment, hard work, compassion, and much more. Our schools need also to go beyond the teaching of subjects and courses. We need to ask what skills and abilities every student should possess as he or she approaches adulthood. Thus, schools should systematically teach and assess competencies as well as courses. Harvard professor Tony Wagner, in his book *Making the Grade,* has suggested a list that makes sense and is a good start for every school to accept, revise, or build upon. He suggests the following four categories of student competencies:

WORKPLACE COMPETENCIES

- Completing one or more work internships
- Solving a complex problem using teamwork
- Using technology to organize and present information relevant to solving a problem
- Analyzing a problem using statistics, trend data, and probability
- Writing a postgraduate work or study plan and preparing a resume
- Developing leadership skills

COMPETENCIES FOR LIFELONG LEARNING

- Presenting, both orally and in writing, an independent research project

- Passing a test on the key features of a geographic map of the world
- Filling out a timeline of important events in history and analyzing an important event in history from multiple points of view
- Demonstrating understanding of the scientific method
- Filling out a 1040 tax form, creating a household budget, and opening a checking account
- Passing a second language proficiency test

CITIZENSHIP COMPETENCIES

- Completing a community service project
- Registering to vote
- Demonstrating an understanding of an important current issue
- Passing a proficiency test on the principles of democratic government

COMPETENCIES FOR PERSONAL GROWTH AND HEALTH

- Completing an independent artistic or musical project
- Demonstrating proficiency in a lifelong sport
- Passing a proficiency test on basic principles of human health
- Demonstrating contemporary life skills

A curriculum based on formal study as well as practical application should address these topics in age- and grade-appropriate ways from the earliest elementary school grades through high school.

To achieve the approaches described above requires good, qualified teachers. Although there are many such educators teaching in inner-city, high-poverty, African-American schools, there are simply not enough to make a real impact. School districts need to take actions to make teaching in these communities attractive and rewarding. As was detailed in the previous chapter, unfortunately most of our brightest college students perceive the teaching profession as one that is not attractive and not rewarding. They are smart enough to add and subtract numbers.

The average teacher starting salary in 2010 was $39,000 a year. If we roughly calculate benefits, and federal and state tax deductions for that amount, their take-home pay would be approximately between $26,000 and $29,000. College seniors in 2010 had an average student loan debt of $25,250. It's not hard to see why so many don't see teaching as an attractive option. Add to the those numbers the way teachers are paid in the majority of school districts because of union contracts, and it becomes apparent the very best, hard working, talented, and committed teachers will earn the exact same amount of money as the unprepared, laziest, uncommitted teachers if they all possess the same degree and have taught the same number of years. No ambitious, talented, young man or woman will find teaching at all appealing, and teaching in a tough, inner-city school without being recognized for one's abilities and hard work is a very difficult selling proposition to make to college seniors. A system that makes no distinctions between excellence, mediocrity, and incompetence goes against the very values we profess when we aspire to realize the American Dream.

The preparation and abilities of too many teachers in our lowest achieving inner-city minority schools is a serious problem that every school district must address if we are to begin to close the black-white achievement gap. The evidence of whether black teachers make any difference in raising academic score in these schools is mixed. Our major urban centers have large percentages of their teaching force who are minorities, yet the low academic achievement of students and high dropout rates would seem to discount the race of the teacher as an important aspect pertaining to student achievement. There is no doubt we need more able and talented African-American teachers but primarily as role models as opposed to a belief that the race of any teacher will lead to scores improving. And we should not forget that the academic success of Asian students is occurring with only a minute percentage of Asian teachers in our schools. We need also recall that no other racial or ethnic group is today arguing that teachers representing their group will raise academic achievement.

The real issue is the preparation and quality of those teaching in our inner-city schools. For too many, the research reveals that they are not ready to step into a classroom just because they have a college degree. California has a basic educational skills test that every prospective teacher must pass; twenty other states have similar assessments. In California 80 percent of white teachers have been passing the first time they take the test, but only 35 percent of African-Americans are passing on their first attempt. This, of course, is an indictment of inadequate education at the elementary and secondary levels, as well as incredibly low standards at universities that enroll them and grant them college degrees. If affirmative action policies allowed even one of those individuals to enter college and graduate, who will measure the academic harm they will inflict on those they teach? A similar sad tale is found in Illinois. The proportion of teachers who failed the Illinois test was four times as high in Chicago as it was in other districts that had fewer minority students and high test scores. In the entire state of Illinois 8 percent of teachers failed at least one area of teacher competence required on the test, but in five minority, high-poverty, districts the average failure rate was 20 percent. In twelve Chicago schools 40 percent of the teachers had failed one or more of the tests. In one infamous case one teacher employed in a Chicago school had failed in twenty-four of twenty-five attempts to pass the test, including all twelve tests in her subject matter. We can only pray for the students in her class.

In high-poverty schools one in four classes is taught by someone who has no formal background in that particular subject; some researchers claim that the real figure is three times that rate. In high-poverty schools about 22 percent of core classes, such as English, history, math, and science, are taught by teachers with no major in the subject matter. The figure for low-poverty schools, while still not good, is about 11 percent. And young, first-year teachers just out of college are assigned to teach in high-poverty schools at two times the rate they are assigned to low-poverty schools. So why, given all the above statistics, should we be surprised that 50 percent of teachers in many urban areas leave their jobs within the first five years of employment?

Quality teachers are badly needed in inner-city African-American schools, but we also need teachers who understand the environments, backgrounds, and culture of the students they teach. When students are asked what one thing would make school better for them, more than 60 percent answered, "having more good teachers." Sixty-nine percent of students said they would learn more from teachers who treated them with respect. Respect, of course, goes both ways, and that is why, as was mentioned previously, character education must teach students that they will receive respect when they simultaneously give respect. Research has also revealed a clear difference in perceptions about their teachers from students of different races. Pedro A. Noguera, in his book *The Trouble With Black Boys*, stressed the point that only a small percentage of black boys and girls feel that they are supported or cared about by their teachers. Because of these student opinions, whether they are accurate or not, our teachers need special training in conveying explicit and implicit messages that they truly believe in the capacity of their students to be successful in school and in life.

Inner-city, low-achieving African-American schools can address these teacher issues in a number of ways. They can insist on having qualified men and women teaching what they are competent to teach. There are only a few ways to get this done. First, school boards must negotiate contracts with teacher unions that give school principals the sole authority to hire whomever they want as long as that candidate is fully qualified. But hiring authority is not enough. Second, school boards must take the lead in negotiating teacher contracts that have clear requirements and guidelines for a performance-based evaluation and compensation system. This should be a collaborative effort by boards of education and teacher unions, but boards must insist that whether or not having such a system is a non-negotiable item. Released from the restrictions of a step-system pay model, boards should then offer teachers appropriate but perhaps different salaries according to conditions in the current educational market. Thus, if science, math, and special education teachers are scarce, they should be offered more money than those persons who teach in areas with an abundance of potential candidates. Small signing bonuses would also aid in attracting good people.

So, too, would a relaxation, or preferably an abandonment, of teacher certification requirements. While there is strong evidence that teacher quality has a major impact on student achievement, there is little evidence that teacher certification has any relation to teacher quality or to high levels of student academic achievement. Of more than 170 research studies on teacher certification, only nine found any significant positive relationship between certification and student academic performance. A small number of five studies actually showed a statistically significant negative effect in that relationship. We should not forget or ignore the fact that the overwhelming number of teachers currently teaching in some of the worse performing schools and school districts in the nation are fully certified teachers. At the high school level a relaxation of certification requirements would open the doors of instruction to a wealth of talent from both the public and private sectors—persons who could serve as role models to young people as well as provide them with specialized information and practical experience normally not available through traditionally trained and certified teachers. A faculty with adjunct teachers who are law enforcement people, scientists, businessmen, anthropologists, museum curators, or book authors would make our inner-city schools centers of new excitement for young people.

There are a number of other issues that schools can and should directly address. In many inner-city African-American schools, students are part of peer groups that devalue education. Many students are subjected to pressure from their peers not to excel in school. This has been labeled an oppositional culture in which academic achievement is viewed as a rejection of one's racial identity. Students are discouraged from doing well in school because they risk the charge that they are "acting white"; they are forced to choose between doing well in school or having friends. Where such attitudes exist, the schools need to address them head on. Student forums should be held in which prominent, educated, and successful African-American men and women talk with students about this issue with the overall theme and message being, "Doing well in school is not acting white, it's acting smart for your future." Or more directly, "Being Black and Failing in School Isn't Cool. It's Being Black and Stupid." Unless schools have such open and honest discussions, too many young black people will never achieve what they are capable of achieving because of the powerful negative influence of their peers.

Schools also need to look at their calendars and school structures. Vocational education has fallen into disfavor in recent decades because some viewed it as a way to discourage some students from going to college; very often those students were African-American. This has been a serious disservice to students and to the nation. Clearly not everyone needs to or should go to college, but in today's world, everyone should go into some kind of post-secondary technical or career training. Schools and school counselors need to promote and encourage this by establishing vocational and career-themed schools as well as counseling students to see the multiple options for a career and decent living standard that are open to them. Schools need to provide the special services needed for students who truly are in the special education category, but they should stop identifying and classifying excessive numbers of black students who are too quickly labeled as special education students, when their problems may be identified and remedied by good counseling and academic tutoring.

If discrimination, poverty, and racial isolation have combined to create a specific subculture that is characterized by anti-middle-class values and lifestyles, then the role of parents in closing the achievement gap is crucial. It is naïve to believe that schools can do much to create a new wave of parental enthusiasm and participation in the schools. Today lifestyles, single-family households, women in the workforce, and geographic dispersion of residences all combine to work against extensive parental involvement. The increasing complexity and difficulty of school subject matter at both the elementary and secondary levels allows only a small percentage of college-educated adults to assist children with their homework or studies. Programs for parents should be offered to inner-city black parents on parenting skills and parenting issues, as well as skill development, literacy, basic math, computer use, and positive discipline for their children.

How schools structure their school year and grade sequence is also important. Studies have presented strong evidence that the September-to-June school year makes little sense in the twenty-first century. Various options are available for districts to adopt twelve-month school calendars that would reduce the academic "loss" that students experience over the summer months in a traditional school calendar and that substantially contribute to closing the achievement gap.

Preschool is very important and can do much to compensate for the lack of resources and time spent by children in the company of adults during the crucial ages from three to five. A large number of African-American inner-city children come to kindergarten or first grade unable to identify colors, letters, or numbers; they lack the ability to relate successfully to other children or to adult authority figures. The importance of early childhood education is by now well documented and accepted, yet overall implementation of these programs is dangerously slow. The catch-up time required by these young unprepared children often keeps them from ever achieving at the level of their innate ability. But the will to act seems to not exist. The question most often asked is how can we afford large-scale preschool programs when we have hardly enough money for the K-12 grades of education?

Here is where a bold step should be contemplated. In surveys of American high school students, a large number classify their senior year as one of limited value and, for some, a clear waste of time. Many students have already completed the requirements needed for graduation, and in many urban inner-city African-American communities, half or more of the students who started as freshmen in high school have dropped out of school and never make it to their senior year. Yet if these dropouts had been given a better start when they began their schooling in kindergarten or first grade, it is likely they would not have fallen further and further behind until, in frustration, they walked away from school completely. One solution would be to make a grade and financial trade, that is, condense the high school program into three years and use the funds previously allocated for the senior year to mandate and finance preschool in our low achieving inner-city minority communities. This would be an investment that would pay huge dividends in reducing later dropout rates and in closing the achievement gap. At minimum, such a program should be done on a pilot basis. Educators talk incessantly about things that are research-based, yet few school policies are actually based on that research, as was evidenced in our discussion regarding the necessity for teachers to be certified. In regard to the importance of early education, the research is extensive and convincing—students who are prepared to start out well in school will have a greater chance of succeeding in school over the long run.

The black student academic failure and dropout rate in our high schools has reached crisis proportions, and schools need to think differently about how our secondary schools are structured. Students should be given opportunities for internships and work-study programs that will allow them to see the practical applications of their school learning to the outside world. If such programs extend the length of the high school years for graduation by one or two years, so be it. The long term cost to our society will be far less than the price we will continue to pay for school dropouts, unemployed citizens, and welfare recipients, and the costs of incarcerating persons who are perpetrators of crime and violence.

Finally, there are those who advocate closing the black-white achievement gap by adopting teaching-learning styles that are particularly unique and successful with African-American children. The assumption here is, interestingly, not that black children be given equal treatment but, rather, that they be given special treatment. For example, advocates of this specialized teaching have said that African-Americans learn better when the teacher mixes activities and switches back and forth between tasks rather than focusing on one task at a time for a long period. It is also argued that black children do better in classes that involve physical movement or when there is music in the background. Others claim that black students need to work more in teams than individually and require more time in class for talking. Few of these claims are based on extensive accepted research but nevertheless should not be too quickly dismissed.

Much more extensive research is needed about this concept as well as variations in learning styles. We cannot simply assume that all humans, of every race and ethnicity, are exactly the same and that they all process information in exactly the same manner. Once again, this is not to say that any one group is superior, only that human differences do exist. Thus, the American educational system, created and developed by Caucasians of European origin, may or may not be best suited to the learning styles of persons of different backgrounds. The truth is, we simply don't know, and many questions remain. If, for example, there is a particular Asian learning style that differs from the current American model, Asian students do not seem to have been adversely affected with poor achievement levels. Most likely, the problems surrounding the achievement gap are not about any particular learning style of African-American students but, rather, unimaginative, outdated school policies, structures, and methods of instruction that are boring and irrelevant daily school practices that impact all American students, regardless of race or ethnicity. Better teachers teaching in creative ways that actively engage students would raise the achievement levels of all students.

The role of schools and school districts in taking concrete steps to close the achievement gap is large. A number of things can and should be done. Many actions will not be easy, and some will stir great controversy. But the stakes are high for the nation, and political and educational leadership is needed now more than ever. America continues to have a great and proud record of educational achievement. The continuing disparity between the academic achievement of black and white students cannot be allowed to be the nation's Achilles Heel. There is much that can and must be done to close that achievement gap. The only question is whether or not we possess the courage and will to act.

CHAPTER XII

SOME FINAL THOUGHTS AND UNANSWERED QUESTIONS

I n our attempt to discover the basic cause or causes of the black-white achievement gap in America, we have stressed certain key historical points. All of American education is in need of some fundamental restructuring because it has become a victim of what sociologists would call cultural lag. The politics, economics, demographics, and technological changes of the early twenty-first century have now left the schools behind, unable to respond to these powerful and fast-moving global forces. Yet while overall change is needed, it is a mistake to label the United States educational system a failure. As we have seen, the schools are working well for many; it is for poor and minority children that our schools are particularly failing. However, we have also reviewed the story of poor and minority students of a previous generation whom the schools also failed, those black migrants who came to the urban North and the scores of immigrants who came to America from eastern and southern Europe. So, contrary to what some may believe, there really was no magical golden era in the past history of American education.

Our quest for answers has also given us some insight into possible explanations for the black-white achievement gap. We have seen that while schools educating black students were not provided with adequate funds in the past, that case cannot be made today, and we have cited examples of urban centers where a great deal of money has made no impact on closing the achievement gap. Our review of poverty revealed that it definitely is a key ingredient in explaining the academic achievement disparity among students, but we have also reviewed the fact that groups other than African-Americans experienced great poverty in the past and yet were able, within a generation, to have their children succeed in school and beyond. But we have also noted that even in non-poverty situations the achievement levels of black students continues to lag behind whites. The historical record also shows that racism was a powerful negative force that affected virtually every African-American, but we also saw that the black experience of being targets of racism was not unique to them. Numerous other groups have been targeted as well, and each of those other groups does not continue to suffer its residual effects either in our schools or in our society.

As we have seen, the impact of family structure has been a major contributor as an underlying factor of the black achievement gap because of the very large percentage of single-parent households and out-of-wedlock births to young and minimally educated girls and women. But we have also recounted the fact that even in previous decades when a high proportion of African-American households were two-parent families, the achievement of their children still remained behind white students. The review of the importance and impact of genetics on the achievement issue made clear that there is no evidence that intellectual inferiority can be used to explain the low achievement of black students and that IQ tests and results are subject to change over time. The record shows that other non-black minorities were labeled inferior and retarded at first, yet their offspring have often become intellectual and economic leaders in our nation.

Having seen that each of these potential explanations has varying degrees of merit and importance in explaining the achievement gap and that other non-black groups have overcome them, one key point must be made regarding African-Americans: **No other racial or ethnic group in America has experienced all of these obstacles for such a consistently long period of time.** The first Africans were brought to our shores in 1619. Even using an arbitrary date of 1965 as a high point in the success of the Civil Rights Movement, it means that for almost 350 years black Americans were subjected to virtually all of the obstacles to success we have reviewed. Once again, to repeat—no other racial or ethnic group has experienced this, let alone been part of a system of slavery that lasted more than 200 years. Given this history, the fact that in the past forty years two-thirds of African-Americans are now part of the middle class is a remarkable achievement. So history is important and cannot be discounted, but neither can it be used as a constant, never-ending excuse.

Our review of the evidence led us finally to the concept of culture and particularly the multifaceted, mostly negative combination of elements that are described as the culture of poverty. It was all the previous causes of the achievement gap we reviewed that combined to create this particular culture, which is perhaps the major causal factor explaining the achievement gap. If, then, this specific culture is a key cause of the achievement gap, logic would lead us to believe that a key to closing the gap would be a program or process to change this unique culture. Once again the historical past teaches that the only way such a change will occur over a long period of time is to create conditions of economic stability, solid families, and the acceptance of American middle-class values. This will not be quick nor will it be easy, so those who are looking for an immediate fix have already been disappointed. The historical record is clear—each minority group succeeded in schools only when primarily two-parent families achieved some measure of economic stability. That is why those who blame the schools and teachers alone for African-American underachievement need to rethink their accusations and read their history, and both our policy makers and our schools must take action.

It is clear that how teachers are prepared in universities is totally inadequate for high-poverty minority schools. No one who receives a university diploma yet cannot pass a basic skills test for teacher certification should be allowed to teach. Nevertheless, we continue to place unprepared individuals in our neediest schools, and, because of teacher union rules, incompetent teachers are rarely terminated.

Our biggest obstacle, outside of school practices themselves, is an education cartel. A cartel is defined as a combination of enterprises or organizations designed to limit competition. This cartel is a combination of university colleges of education, teachers unions, school board associations, and school administrator groups, each working to protect or advance their own adult organizational interests. This is not some clandestine organized conspiracy; each group operates separately, yet the combined separate actions represent one massive blockage to the needed changes that could close the achievement gap. Each organization says exactly the right things—that their sole mission is to do what's best for children—yet their actions, policies, and political actions tell a different story. When one gets to the core of their positions, it is too often not what is best for kids but rather what is best for each of their particular adult constituencies. Each lobbies legislatures to make or stop proposed changes, but none of these groups has presented a serious workable agenda to address the persistent underachievement of our African-American students. We clearly lack educational leadership that would bring these groups together and ask, What are each of you proposing to do to raise the quality of our schools and of education in our African-American underachieving communities? What will your group contribute? What will your group give up? What are you going to do that you haven't done before to close the achievement gap? At this point that necessary leadership is absent, and the need for joint educator action is greater than ever before.

Educators must not allow public policy regarding schools to be driven only by legislators at the local, state, and federal levels. Without serious input, lobbying, and even resistance by professional educators, we will continue to get unrealistic and flawed legislative mandates, such as the No Child Left Behind law, which has failed to improve education of children and has done more to demoralize communities and drive good people out of education than any legislation in American history. Two hypothetical exercises can illustrate the point.

Let's assume that a law was passed that specified that by the year 2025 every player on every major league baseball team should achieve a 400 batting average. Targets were established so that by 2015 everyone should achieve a 300 batting average and that by 2020 everyone should be batting 350 and that by 2025 all will be required to bat 400. Let's further assume that every player, regardless of whether he suffers from some mental or physical disability, must reach that batting average goal. And let's assume even further that if the team did not reach that collective goal by 2025, the team would be eliminated from major league baseball. How much money would you be willing to wager that the policy would succeed?

Or let's take another scenario. Let's assume that a law was passed that required every city in America to have no citizens at the poverty level by 2025. Here, too, targets would be set. By 2015, for example, everyone's earned income must reach one-quarter of the established poverty level, by 2020 their income must reach one-half of the poverty level, by 2022 that income must be at three-fourths of the poverty level, and by 2025 every single adult person in that city must be earning income at or above the poverty level. And let's further assume that the law applied to everyone, regardless of whether they could read or write; or could speak or read English; or had any mental, emotional, or physical disabilities. It applied to adults of any age. The law would also require that if a given city did not meet these requirements, citizens could move elsewhere, or the city would be shut down. How much money would you be willing to wager that this public policy would succeed?

The above scenarios, while clearly ridiculous, are not too much more ridiculous than the requirements of the No Child Left Behind federal education mandates. This policy, like the two fictional examples, is based on the unattainable goal of equality of results, not our nation's historic value and goal of equality of opportunity. This very real policy also claims that every child, even those with mental, emotional, and physical challenges, will meet the goal of reading and math achievement by 2014 and that students must achieve certain levels of proficiency at specific years from the time the legislation was enacted until every single child in the United States of America achieves this magic level by 2014. The safest bet you will ever make will be to bet against this goal ever being met.

So in 2014 the results will be that the achievement gap will not be closed; communities will have been stigmatized for having failing schools, even though their students might have shown continued academic growth from very low starting points; and thousands of teachers will have left the profession, or not even entered it, because of the pressure to abandon their passion and creativity for teaching our young so that our schools could become testing factories. This is why, as the NCLB legislation slowly is ignored, reformed, or repealed, it will be remembered as perhaps the most ill-conceived and unsuccessful piece of federal education legislation ever passed.

Important questions regarding the black-white achievement gap are still unanswered. As we have seen, some statistics are troubling and call for further inquiry. The fact that in every state in our nation black students are underperforming is not quickly or easily answered by a "culture of poverty" explanation. The fact is that not all of these children in every single state in our country are living in poverty conditions. The fact that white students outperform black students from families who are poor, or middle class, or upper class is also troubling and also calls for serious additional research. What additional knowledge must we acquire to explain the underachievement of black students in Canada, Europe, Australia, and South America? Why are they underperforming there as well? We cannot use the historical experience of America as an explanation or excuse for the academic performance of those students. We need also to probe more deeply into the fact that Caribbean blacks and African immigrants to our country do so much better in our schools than our native-born African-American students.

The research of scholars in the fields of learning, cognition, and personal success is also raising important issues and questions that will impact the very definition of what the word *achievement* actually means. Currently, we mean the word to describe the level of success students reach on certain standardized tests. The gap is the difference between black and white students on state tests or the National Assessment of Educational Progress (NAEP) or on the ACT and SAT. But the work that has been done on Multiple Intelligences and Emotional Intelligence should force us to rethink the high stakes, high pressure environment we have created for students and teachers when, in fact, those tests may have little to do with identifying the potential future success of our students. Paul Tough, in his book, *How Children Succeed*, reviews research currently being done that is revealing a very different path to success. In reviewing what these researchers are finding, Tough says, "What matters most in a child's development, they say, is not how much information we can stuff into her brain in the first few years. What matters, instead, is whether we are able to help her develop a very different set of qualities, a list that includes persistence, self-control, curiosity, conscientiousness, grit, and self-confidence." Tough says these attributes can be classified under different names but essentially they are part of what we describe as a person's character.

This does not mean that schools should de-emphasize math, reading, science, and history, only that we should not continue to exert this incredible pressure on schools to achieve higher and higher test scores or be publicly penalized, embarrassed, or shut down. These academically failing schools need help, not just threats of punishment, and parents and students need choice and options rather than being forced to attend unsuccessful monopolies, which in the private sector would quickly be out of business. Of course, students need to be periodically tested so that we have some record of what they have learned, but so, too, should we develop assessments for those other attributes that author Paul Tough described as real indicators of potential student success.

Finally, we must dig much deeper into the relationship and interaction of different cultures to a student's ability to be academically successful in school. Why is it, for example, that Caribbean blacks have fared so well in American schools but have done so poorly in Canadian and English schools? If, as we have argued, the key to success in our schools is for students to follow American middle-class values, why is it that the children of middle-class African-Americans still fall behind white students in academic achievement levels? Why is it that Asian students from different Asian countries have such different academic success rates in American schools? Why is it that in England students of Greek origin fall academically behind, yet these same students of Greek origin reach very high achievement levels in Germany, Australia, and the United States? These are intriguing questions that await serious further research that could give us more precise insights into the black-white achievement gap in our own country.

So questions remain that should be investigated, but we cannot wait for all these answers to be found. Our nation cannot afford to wait as another generation of young African-Americans does not reach its God-given potential utilizing the full range of their talents. The great American educational reformer and leader Horace Mann stated an important truth in saying, "Education, then, beyond all other devices of human origin, is the great equalizer of the conditions of man, the balance wheel of the social machinery." That insight is even truer today than it was in the nineteenth century. The black-white achievement gap need not be American education's Achilles Heel. We can avoid that fate if we accept the challenge of the problem and display a leadership of action.

BIBLIOGRAPHY

Abada, Teresa, Hou, Feng and Ram, Bali—"Ethnic Differences in Educational Attainment Among the Children of Canadian Immigrants"—*Canadian Journal of Sociology*, Vol 34, 2009

Almay, Sarah & Theohas, Christina—*Not Prepared for Class: High Poverty Schools Continue to Have Fewer In-Field Teachers*—The Education Trust, November 2010

Amin, Kaushika; Demack, Sean, Drew, David; Fosam, Bekia, Gilliborn, David—*Black and Ethnic Minority Young People and Educational Disadvantage*—London, England: The Runnymede Trust, 1997

Auletta, Ken—*The Underclass*—New York: Vintage Books, 1983

Bennett, William J.—*The Index of Leading Cultural Indicators*—New York: Broadway Books, 1999

Bracey, Gerald W.—*What you Should Know About The War Against America's Public Schools*—Boston: Allyn and Bacon, 2003

Buchanan, Patrick J—*Suicide of a Superpower*—New York: St. Martin Press, 2011

Carter, Samuel Casey—*No Excuses, Lessons from 21 High Performing High-Poverty Schools*—Washington D.C.: The Heritage Foundation, 2001

Chenoweth, Karen—*It's Being Done: Academic Success in Unexpected Schools*—Cambridge Mass: Harvard Education Press, 2008

Clark, Reginald M.—*Family Life and School Achievement: Why Poor Black Children Succeed or Fail*—Chicago: University of Chicago Press, 1983

Coontz, Stephanie—*The Way We Never Were: Americas Families and the Nostalgia Trap*—New York: Basic Books, 1992

Fase, William—*Ethnic Divisions in Western European Education*—New York: Waxman Munster, 1994

Fullen, Michael—*Turnaround Leadership*—San Francisco: Jossey-Boss, 2006

Gardner, Howard—*Multiple Intelligences: The Theory in Practice*—New York: Basic Books, 1993

Goleman, Daniel—*Emotional Intelligence: Why it can matter more than IQ*—New York: Bantam Books, 1995

Goodhart, David—*Inner-city cultures to blame for London riots*—http://globalpublicsquare.blogs.cnn.com/2011/08/11

Greene, Jay P.—*Education Myths, What Special Interest Groups Want You To Believe About Our Schools—And Why it Isn't So*—Lanham, Maryland: Rowman and Littlefield, 2005

Greer, Colin—*The Great School Legend*—New York: Viking Press, 1972

Gross, Martin L.—*The Conspiracy of Ignorance: The Failure of American Public Schools*—New York: Harper Collins, 1999

Hacher, Andrew—*Two Nations: Black and White, Separate, Hostile, Unequal*—New York: Scribner, 2003

Hale-Benson, Janice E.—*Black Children: Their Roots, Culture, and Learning Styles*—Baltimore: The Johns Hopkins University Press, 1982

Harrison, Laurence—*Who Prospers: How Cultural Values Shape Economic and Political Success*—New York: Basic Books, 1992

Harrison, Laurence & Huntington, Samuel—*Culture Matters: How Values Shape Human Progress*—New York: Basic Books, 2000

Herrnstein, Richard J. & Murray, Charles—*The Bell Curve: Intelligence and Class Structure in American Life*—New York: Free Press, 1994

Herskovits, Melville J.—*The myth of the Negro Past*—Boston: Beacon Press, 1990

Homel, Michael W.—*Down From Equality: Black Chicagoans and the Public Schools, 1920-1941*—Urbana: University of Illinois Press, 1984

Huffington, Ariana—*Third World America*—New York: Crown Publishing Group, 2010

Jencks, Christopher & Peterson, Paul E., ed.—*The Urban Underclass*—Washington D.C: The Brookings Institute, 1991

Jencks, Christopher & Phillips, Meredith, ed.—*The Black-White Test Score Gap*—Brookings Institute Press, 1998

Kahlenberg, Richard D.—*The Future of School Integration: Socioeconomic Diversity as an Education Reform Strategy*—Washington DC: The Century Foundation, 2012

Kahlenberg, Richard D.—"Learning from James Coleman"—Washington D.C.: *The Public Interest*, Summer 2001

Katz, Michael B, ed.—*The Underclass Debate: Views from History*—Princeton New Jersey: Princeton University Press, 1993

Kochman, Thomas—*Black & White Styles in Conflict*—Chicago: University of Chicago Press, 1981

Luciak, Mikael—*The Educational Situation of Migrants and Ethnic Minorities in 15 EU Member States in Comparative Perspective*—http://www.inst.at/trans/15nr/08_i/luciak15.htm

Luciak, Mikael—"Minority Status and Schooling—John U. Ogbu's Theory and The schooling of ethnic minorities in Europe"—*Intercultural Education*, Vol 15, No 4, 2004

Mayer, Susan E.—*What Money Can't Buy: Family Income and Children's Life Chances*—Cambridge Mass: University Press, 1997

Murray, Charles—*Coming Apart: The State of White America, 1960-2010*—New York: Crown Publishing Group, 2012

Murray, Charles—*Losing Ground: American Social Policy 1950-1980*—New York: Basic Books, 1984

Murray, Charles—*Real Education*—New York: Crown Publishing Group, 2008

Nasaw, David—*Schooled To Order: A Social History of Public Schooling in The United States*—New York: Oxford University Press, 1979

Necherman, Kathryn M.—*Schools Betrayed: Roots of Failure in Inner-City Education*—Chicago: University of Chicago Press, 2007

Nisbett, Richard E.—*Intelligence and How To Get It: Why Schools and Culture Matter*—New York: W.W. Norton, 2009

Noguera, Pedro—*The Trouble with Black Boys*—San Francisco: Jossey-Bass, 2008

Ogbu, John V.—*Black American Students in an Affluent Suburb: A Study of Academic Disengagement*—Mahwah, New Jersey: Laurence Erlbaum Associates, 2003

Ogbu, John V.—"Minority Education in Comparative Perspective"—*Journal of Negro Education*, Vol 59, No 1 1990

Open Society Institute—*Education for Migrant, Minority, and Marginalized Children in Europe*—Payne, Ruby K.; DeVol, Philip; Smith, Terie Dreussi—*Bridges out of Poverty*—Highland, Texas: AHA! Process, 2001

Payne, Ruby—*A Framework for Understanding Poverty*—Highland, Texas: AHA! Process, 2005

Perlmann, Joel—*Ethnic Differences: Schooling and Social Structure among the Irish, Italians, Jews, and Blacks in an American City, 1880-1935*—New York, Cambridge University Press, 1989

Ravitch, Diane—*The Death and Life of the Great American School System*—New York: Basic Books, 2010

Ravitch, Diane—*Left Back, A Century of Failed School Reform*—New York: Simon & Schuster, 2000

Ravitch, Diane—*The Schools We Deserve: Reflections on The Educational Crises of our Time*—New York: Basic Books, 1985

Ravitch, Diane—*The Troubled Crusade: American Education, 1945-1980*—New York: Basic Books, 1983

Rockefeller Philanthropy Advisors—*Strong American Schools*—Washington D.C. 2008

Rollock, Nicola—*Failure by Any Other Name: Educational Policy and the Continuing Struggle for Black Academic Success*—London, England: The Runnymede Trust, 2007

Rothstein, Richard—*Class and Schools: Using Social, Economic and Educational Reform to Close the Black-White Achievement Gap*—Washington D.C: Economic Policy Institute, 2004

Sandel, Michael – *What Money Can't Buy: The Moral Limits Of Markets*—New York, Farrar, Straus and Giroux, 2012

Sawhill, Isabel V.—*The Behavioral Aspects of Poverty*—Washington D.C.: The Public Interest, Fall 2003

Skandera, Hanna & Sousa, Richard—*School Figures: The Data Behind the Debate*—Stanford, California: Hoover Institution Press, 2003

Sowell, Thomas—*Black, Redneck and White Liberals*—New York: Encounter Books, 2006

Sowell, Thomas—*Economic Facts and Fallacies*—New York: Basic Books, 2007

Sowell, Thomas—*The Economics and Politics of Race: An International Perspective*—New York: William Morrow, 1983

Sowell, Thomas—*Education: Assumptions Versus History*—Stanford, California: Hoover Institution Press, 1986

Sowell, Thomas—*Ethnic America: A History*—New York: Basic Books, 1981

Sowell, Thomas—*Inside American Education*—New York: The Free Press, 1993

Sowell, Thomas—*Race & Culture: A World View*—New York: Basic Books, 1994

Spear, Allan H.—*Black Chicago: The Making of a Negro Ghetto 1890-1920*—Chicago: University of Chicago Press, 1967

Steinberg, Laurence—*Beyond the Classroom: Why School Reform has Failed and What Parents Can Do*—New York: Simon & Schuster, 1996

Steinberg, Stephen—*The Ethnic Myth: Race, Ethnicity, and Class in America*—New York: Athenaeum, 1981

Thernstrom, Stephan & Abigail—*America in Black and White*—New York: Simon & Schuster, 1997

Thernstrom, Stephan & Abigail—No *Excuses: Closing the Racial Achievement Gap*—New York: Simon & Schuster, 2003

Thompson, Gail L.—*Through Ebony Eyes: What Teachers Need to Know But Are Afraid To Ask About African-American Children*—San Francisco: Jossey-Boss, 2004

Tough, Paul—*How Children Succeed*—New York: Houghton Mifflin Harcourt, 2012

Tyack, David B.—*The One Best System: A History of American Urban Education*—Cambridge, Mass: Harvard University Press, 1974

Vegas, Emilia & Petrow, Jenny—*Raising Student Learning in Latin America: The Challenge for the 21st Century*—Washington D.C, The World Bank, 2008

Wagner, Tony—*The Global Achievement Gap*—New York: Basic Books, 2008

Wagner, Tony—*Making the Grade: Reinventing America's Schools*—New York: Routledge Falmer, 1997

Weissberg, Robert—*Bad Students, Not Bad Schools*—New Brunswick, New Jersey: Transaction Publishers, 2010

Wilson, William Julius—*More than Just Race: Being Black and Poor in The Inner City*—New York: W.W. Norton, 2009

Wilson, William Julius—*When Work Disappears: The World of the Urban Poor*—New York: Vintage Books, 1996